Using Clocks and Calendars

Level 3 – Level 5

JANE ELLIS
LUCY PODDINGTON

CONTENTS

🕐 Introduction 3

🕐 Unit 1: Clocks, Watches and Timers

Level 3 5
Level 4 13
Level 5 23
Generic Sheets 30

🕐 Unit 2: Calendars and Diaries

Level 3 35
Level 4 41
Level 5 50
Generic Sheets 55

🕐 Unit 3: Timelines and Timetables

Level 3 61
Level 4 71
Level 5 83
Generic Sheets 91

🕐 Pupil Assessment Sheet 96

Published by Hopscotch Educational Publishing Ltd,
29 Waterloo Place, Leamington Spa CV32 5LA.
(Tel: 01926 744227)

© 2002 Hopscotch Educational Publishing Ltd

Produced for Hopscotch Educational Publishing Ltd by Bender Richardson White, Uxbridge

Devised and planned by Jane Ellis

Activity sheets created by Lucy Poddington

Edited by Lionel Bender

Page make-up and illustration by Pumpkin House, Cambridge

Cover illustrated by Susan Hutchison

Printed by Stephens and George Ltd

Jane Ellis and Lucy Poddington hereby assert their moral right to be identified as the authors of this work in accordance with the Copyright, Designs and Patents Act, 1988.

National Numeracy Strategy Framework for Teaching
© Crown copyright March 1999

ISBN 1-904307-03-5

All rights reserved. This book is sold subject to the condition that it shall not, by way of trade or otherwise, be lent, hired out or otherwise circulated without the publisher's prior consent in any form or binding or cover other than that in which it is published and without a similar condition, including this condition, being imposed upon the subsequent purchaser.

No part of this publication may be reproduced, stored in a retrieval system, or transmitted, in any form or by any means, electronic, mechanical, photocopying, recording or otherwise, without the prior permission of the publisher, except where photocopying for the educational establishment that has purchased this book is expressly permitted in the text.

INTRODUCTION

ABOUT THE SERIES

Using Classroom Resources is a series of books that provides teachers with lessons using available resources such as money and clocks. While the lessons and activities are taught in line with the requirements of The National Numeracy Strategy's *Framework for Teaching*, there are many additional ideas and activities that enable teachers to broaden the work.

These books are ideal because they offer considerable practice for those children who are struggling to grasp the concepts and skills, while also providing extension activities for those children who have grasped the concepts and skills.

The books are organised into three sections which relate to different aspects of the subject. Within each section are lesson plans and photocopiable activities for the different levels of ability being addressed. At the end of each section are generic sheets that can be used in a variety of ways.

The learning objectives in the series have been linked closely to the National Numeracy Strategy's Framework and the introduction to each level has a strong emphasis on whole-class direct teaching as well as a planned purposeful plenary. Teachers should select from the range of activities given in each level in order to differentiate the work for the ability of their class.

Display ideas are included at the end of each level to help the teacher promote continuous learning through the classroom environment.

ABOUT THIS BOOK

This book aims to:
- provide clear lesson plans that focus on specific learning objectives linked to the children's yearly teaching programme
- support teachers through activity ideas based on whole-class, group, paired and individual learning
- encourage children to link the work to everyday life
- give the children many opportunities to handle clocks, watches, diaries, calendars and timetables in the classroom
- allow children to relate 'time' to their school day, weekends and holidays
- produce fun activities for the children to appreciate the concept of time
- introduce the life-long skills of using a diary or calendar.

LINKS TO THE CURRICULUM

This book contains activities that are organised into the levels that relate to the National Curriculum level descriptions. The expectations in the yearly teaching programmes correspond to these levels:

Year 3: Level 3
Year 4: Revision of Level 3, Level 4
Year 5: Revision of Level 4, start on Level 5
Year 6: Level 5

Content of the National Numeracy Strategy's Framework for Yearly Teaching Programmes
Following are the links to the 'Measures' strand of the Framework.

Year 3
- Read and begin to write the vocabulary related to time.
- Use units of time and know the relationships between them (second, minute, hour, day, week, month, year).
- Suggest suitable units to estimate or measure time.
- Use a calendar.
- Read the time to 5 minutes on an analogue clock and a 12-hour digital clock, and use the notation 9:40.

Year 4
- Use, read and write the vocabulary related to time.
- Estimate/check times using seconds, minutes, hours.
- Read the time from an analogue clock to the nearest minute, and from a 12-hour digital clock.
- Use a.m. and p.m. and the notation 9:53.
- Read simple timetables.
- Use this year's calendar.

Year 5
- Use units of time.
- Read the time on a 24-hour digital clock and use 24-hour clock notation, such as 19:53.
- Use timetables.

Year 6
- Appreciate different times around the world.

These are the expectations for each year group. Skills need to be practised continuously and, therefore, there may be assessment of pre-requisite knowledge in each yearly teaching programme. For example, some objectives from Years 4 and 5 would continue to be assessed in Year 6.

▶ Introduction

UNIT CONTENT

🕒 Learning objectives

The learning objectives give a clear teaching focus for each unit. It is good practice to display and share the learning objectives with the children at the beginning of each lesson.

🕒 Key vocabulary

The majority of the words have been taken from the NNS *Mathematical Vocabulary* book. Ideally these words should also be displayed, and referred to, during the lesson. If there are children with language difficulties, it can be effective to point at the words as they are used.

🕒 Resources

This list is only a suggestion of resources that may be used by the children or teacher. These resources, and others, should be readily available in school.

🕒 Introduction

This outlines how you could introduce and teach the topics and skills the children need to learn in the unit. The emphasis is on whole-class teaching and creating interactive activities through direct teaching.

The direct teaching methods outlined in the National Numeracy Strategy's Framework are:
- directing
- instructing
- demonstrating
- explaining and illustrating
- questioning and discussing
- consolidating
- evaluating the children's responses
- summarising.

🕒 Activity sheets

The activity sheets provide tasks that the children can do more or less independently from the teacher. They are designed to support and reinforce teaching, not replace it. Before the children are given the activity sheets to work on, the teacher should ensure that the whole class has understood the numeracy principles being tested.

The notes introducing each activity sheet give ideas and suggestions for making the most of the sheets. They sometimes make suggestions for the whole-class introduction, the plenary session or follow-up work based on the activity sheet.

🕒 Support

Here are ideas for simplifying the tasks to enable lower-attaining children to have access to the learning objectives. They may involve adapting the activity sheet or one of the generic sheets, using numbers appropriate to the level of attainment.

🕒 Challenge

Here are ideas to extend the content of the activity sheets for higher-attaining children.

🕒 Plenary

These are carefully planned activities to finish a lesson, through reflection and assessment. To be effective, there should be a 10 to 15 minutes' time allowance at the end of the lesson. The emphasis again is on whole-class, interactive teaching. It is good practice to refer back to the learning objective and ask 'What have you learned today?'

🕒 Display opportunity

These ideas will enable the teacher to transfer work from the lesson on to a display board. Children continue to learn through displays, and many suggestions in this book include interactive displays where the teacher can continue to 'teach' through changing questions on the wall.

🕒 Extra activities

Here are additional ideas to help the children achieve the learning objectives. More suggestions are given for adapting and using the activity and generic sheets, but as teachers you will no doubt think of many more!

▶ Clocks, Watches and Timers: Level 3

▶ UNIT 1: CLOCKS, WATCHES AND TIMERS
LEVEL 3

🕐 Learning objectives

- To read the time to 5 minutes on an analogue clock and on a 12-hour digital clock, and use the notation 9:40.
- To begin to use a.m. and p.m. notation.
- To consolidate the vocabulary of time and the relevant abbreviations.
- To solve problems involving time.

Key vocabulary

- hour, minute, second, o'clock, half past, quarter to, quarter past, a.m., p.m., digital/analogue clock/watch

🕐 Resources

- classroom analogue clock
- digital clock
- traditional mechanical clock (with geared mechanism so minute and hour hands move together)
- timers or stopwatches
- balls

🕐 Introduction

- Revise digital times with the class and discuss how many minutes there are in one hour, half an hour, quarter of an hour and three-quarters of an hour. Display a large analogue clock and a large digital clock; show a time (to five minutes) on one and ask a child to make the same time on the other. With the whole class, count aloud in fives up to 60 and back to ensure that all the children are confident with the five times table. Let them practise reading the time to five minutes on both digital and analogue clocks.

🕐 Activities

- **Activity Sheet 1** – For this activity, first ensure that the children understand how to play dominoes. If necessary, show them a set of standard dominoes and explain how to arrange them so that the values on neighbouring dominoes match up. Then explain that the dominoes on the activity page have time values instead of dots. Once they have completed the activity, they could cut out the dominoes, mix them up and try to reassemble them, working in pairs. They could also make more domino games of their own.

- **Activity Sheet 2** – Encourage the children to use a ruler to draw the hands on the analogue clocks. Revise 'a.m.' and 'p.m.' and discuss which of the appointment times will be a.m. times and which will be p.m. times. As an extension activity, ask them to work out how long each appointment lasts. They could write sentences about the appointments using language of time such as 'before', 'after', 'earliest' and 'latest', for example 'Alfie's appointment is half an hour after Phoebe's,' and 'Snuffles's appointment is the earliest.'

- **Activity Sheet 3** – This activity involves adding and subtracting periods of time. Read through the list of Sports Day events with the children and explain that the teacher, Miss Sugden, has made notes for herself to help her organise the day. The children can work in pairs to fill in the gaps (pair weaker readers with fluent ones). They could first note down the finish time of each event to help them solve the problems. They can check their answers by turning the hands of a traditional mechanical clock.

- **Activity Sheet 4** – Before beginning the activity, practise with the whole class finding times that are 35 minutes before/after the current time. Write the times on the board using both analogue and digital notation. The children need to be comfortable with writing digital times. They can check their answers by turning the hands of a traditional mechanical clock.

- **Activity Sheet 5** – This activity involves adding and subtracting periods of time. Revise the vocabulary 'early', 'late', 'earliest' and 'latest', and read the train information with the children. Explain that the time due is the time the train is expected to arrive. They can work in pairs (pair weaker readers with fluent ones). Remind them to include a.m. or p.m. in

▶ Clocks, Watches and Timers: Level 3

their answers for questions 1 to 3. Further questions can be asked based on the information, for example 'If the Newcastle train is running 10 minutes late, what time will it arrive?'

- **Activity Sheet 6** – The children should work in groups of four for this activity. Each group needs a timer or stopwatch and a ball. Explain that they should estimate first how long they think the challenge might take them. Emphasise that the quickest person is the one who takes the least time and the slowest is the one who takes the most time. Revise the term 'difference'. The children could also find the average time, to the nearest second. As an extension activity, make a block graph to show the results for the whole class, using time bands such as 'less than 30 seconds' '30–45 seconds' '45–60 seconds' and so on. Ask questions based on the graph.

Support

Change the instructions on Activity Sheet 4 so that the children have to find the time 30 minutes before/after the time on the clock (or 15 minutes, or one hour, as appropriate). Instead of writing the digital times, they could take it in turns with a partner to make the new time by turning the hands of an analogue clock.

Use Generic Sheet 4 (page 33). Fill in a variety of times to five minutes and ask the children to write the equivalent times.

Challenge

When the children have completed Activity Sheet 1, ask them to glue the page in the centre of a sheet of A3 paper. Working in groups, they can draw more dominoes joining on to the existing set and write or draw appropriate times on them.

Ask them to cut out and collect television listings from magazines or newspapers. They can then solve problems of duration based on these, by working out how long each programme lasts.

Plenary

Split the class into two groups for a quiz. Give each child a small whiteboard or sheet of scrap paper. Call out questions such as 'Group 1: What is 20 minutes after 10:05 a.m.?' The children record their answers and show these to everyone. For every correct answer, award one point for their group. Continue to alternate questions between groups 1 and 2.

Display opportunity

Create a large appointments chart like the one on Activity Sheet 2, or enlarge a blank page from an appointments diary. Laminate the sheet so that it can be wiped clean and reused. Using a scenario such as parents' evening or doctor's appointments, say people's names and the time of their appointment, for example 'Mrs Webb, twenty-five to nine'. Ask children to come to the front and write the appointments on the chart, using digital notation.

Extra activities

Use Generic Sheet 1 (page 30) for matching games. More cards could be made showing other times to five minutes. To make them more durable, copy them on to card and laminate them. Ask the children to work in pairs or small groups. They should take turns to pick a card and find the matching time. Several different games can be played using these cards, for example 'Snap' or a memory game (the cards are spread face down on the table; children take it in turns to turn over two cards. If they match, the child keeps them; if not, the cards are turned back over).

Answers

Activity Sheet 3

9:25 a.m.	9:55 a.m.	10:30 a.m.
45 mins	11:30 a.m.	1 hr 5 mins
12:00 p.m.	30 mins	

Activity Sheet 4

1. 4:40	2. 11:05	3. 7:50	4. 11:25
5. 12:20	6. 3:10	7. 5:55	8. 7:50
9. 5:25	10. 2:55	11. 3:20	12. 8:30

Activity Sheet 5

1. 10:40 a.m.
2. 11:00 a.m.
3. 11:15 a.m.
4. 30 mins
5. Newcastle train
6. Alan – late
   Jamila – on time
   Darren – on time
   Josie – late

Time dominoes

Write the missing times on the dominoes.

 | 10:55

five to ___ |

Remember how dominoes match up.

___ : ___ | twenty-five past two

___ past eight | ___ : ___

7:35 | five past five

12:25 | ___ : ___ |

___ : ___ | ___ four

five ___ ___ ___ |

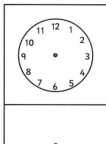 | ___ : ___

twenty-five to eleven | ___ : ___

PHOTOCOPIABLE

Name_____   ▶ Clocks – Activity Sheet 2

Pets at the vet's

The cards show today's appointments at the vet's.
Draw the hands on the clocks.

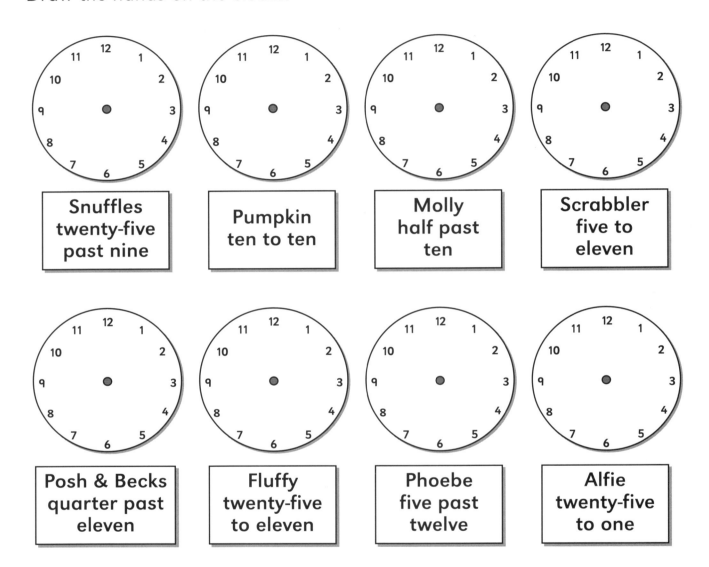

Write the times as digital times. Use a.m. or p.m.

Snuffles _____   Posh & Becks _____

Pumpkin _____   Fluffy _____

Molly _____   Phoebe _____

Scrabbler _____   Alfie _____

PHOTOCOPIABLE
© Hopscotch Educational Publishing 2002

Name_____   ▸ Clocks – Activity Sheet 3

Sports Day

Read the list of Sports Day events.

Event	Start time	Length of event
Sack race	9:45 a.m.	10 mins
Gym display	10:05 a.m.	25 mins
Dressing-up race	10:40 a.m.	10 mins
Penalty shoot-out	10:55 a.m.	35 mins
Relay race	11:35 a.m.	15 mins

Miss Sugden is making notes about Sports Day.

Fill in the gaps.

Arrive 20 mins before the sack race (_____ a.m.).

Sack race ends at _____ a.m.

Gym display ends at _____ a.m.

_____ mins between end of sack race and start of dressing-up race.

Penalty shoot-out ends at _____ a.m.

_____ hr _____ mins between end of gym display and start of relay race.

Lunch 10 mins after end of relay race (_____ p.m.).

Dance display takes twice as long as relay race (_____ mins).

PHOTOCOPIABLE
© Hopscotch Educational Publishing 2002

Clocks – Activity Sheet 4

Time spells

The 'Avanca' spell makes time go forwards 35 minutes.

The 'Retarda' spell makes time go back 35 minutes.

Write the digital time after each spell has been cast.

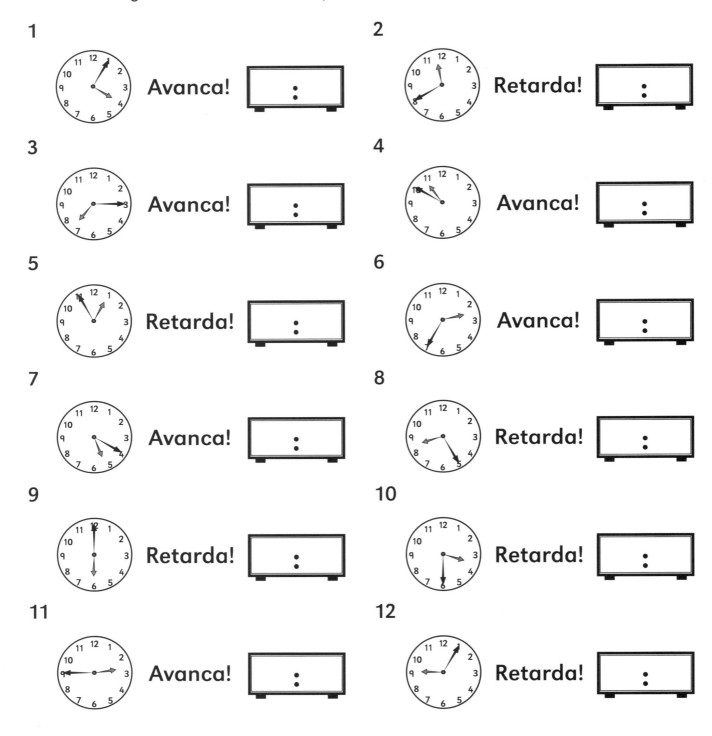

Name_____

▶ Clocks – Activity Sheet 5

All aboard!

It is 10:25 a.m.

Read about the trains stopping at a station.

Train to Wakefield due in 15 mins.
Train to Leeds due in 35 mins.
Train to Huddersfield due in 20 mins.
Train to Newcastle due in 50 mins.
Train to Scarborough due in 45 mins.

Answer the questions.

1   What time is the Wakefield train due? _____

2   What time is the Leeds train due? _____

3   What time is the Newcastle train due? _____

4   How long after the Huddersfield train is the Newcastle train due?
    _____

5   Which is the latest train? _____

6   These people want to catch trains. Are they on time or late for their trains?

Name	Arrives at station	Going to	On time or late?
Alan	10:55 a.m.	Huddersfield	_____
Jamila	10:55 a.m.	Leeds	_____
Darren	11:05 a.m.	Scarborough	_____
Josie	11:20 a.m.	Newcastle	_____

PHOTOCOPIABLE
© Hopscotch Educational Publishing 2002

Name_____   ▶ Clocks – Activity Sheet 6

Timer challenge

Work with three friends. Your challenge is to bounce a ball 20 times each.

First estimate how long it will take you. Then take turns to do it while the others time you. Record your results.

Name	Estimated time	Actual time

Use the chart to help you find the answers.

1   Who was the quickest? _____
2   Who was the slowest? _____
3   What was the total time for all four of you? _____
4   For each person, work out the difference between the estimated time and the actual time.

   Name: _____ _____ _____

   Difference: _____ _____ _____

   Whose estimate was closest? _____
5   How long would it take you to bounce a ball 40 times? _____
6   How long would it take you to bounce a ball 200 times? _____

PHOTOCOPIABLE
© Hopscotch Educational Publishing 2002

▶ Clocks, Watches and Timers: Level 4

▶ UNIT 1: CLOCKS, WATCHES AND TIMERS
LEVEL 4

Learning objectives

- To read the time from an analogue clock to the nearest minute.
- To use a.m. and p.m.
- To read the time on a 24-hour digital clock and use 24-hour clock notation, such as 19:53.
- To solve problems involving time.

Key vocabulary

- hour, minute, second, a.m., p.m., 24-hour clock, 12-hour clock

Resources

- classroom analogue clock
- digital clock
- traditional mechanical clocks
- timers or stopwatches

Introduction

- Use an analogue clock to reinforce that there are 60 minutes in one hour. Set the clock to a variety of times (to the nearest minute) and let the children practise reading the time. Encourage them to write the times using 12-hour digital notation.

- Introduce the 24-hour clock and demonstrate how 24 hours (one day) can be shown on a digital clock. Discuss how 24-hour times are written for analogue clocks, i.e. using a.m. and p.m. Introduce the vocabulary '24-hour clock' and '12-hour clock'. To assess the children's understanding, ask them to read times from 24-hour digital clocks and convert a.m. and p.m. times to 24-hour times (and vice versa).

Activities

- **Activity Sheet 7** – This activity focuses on reading times to the nearest minute on analogue and 12-hour digital clocks. As an extension activity, the children could write a list of digital times and ask a partner to show the matching time on an analogue clock.

- **Activity Sheet 8** – This activity will help to familiarise the children with the 24-hour clock. The mystery phrase is 'digital clock'. Working in groups, the children could make their own sets of cards with 24-hour and a.m./p.m. times for another group to match up.

- **Activity Sheet 9** – This activity provides practice in converting a.m. and p.m. times to 24-hour times and time in words. As an extension activity, the children could work out how long it is between each activity on the chart. Alternatively, you could tell them that Gran is always running late and does all the activities 5 minutes later than planned. Ask them to make a new chart showing the actual times that Gran does the activities.

- **Activity Sheet 10** – The children can work in pairs on this activity. They will need simple timers or stopwatches and extra pieces of paper for carrying out the tasks. Provide resources as necessary to help them complete the tasks, for example a chart of the eight times table, pictures or stencils of regular shapes and non-fiction books or CD-ROMs containing information on frogs. Encourage them to complete the tasks in any order, so that they will not need to use the same resources all at the same time.

- Ask the children to compare their estimates and discuss how close their estimates were, using phrases such as 'Task 1 took less time than we thought,' and 'Task 2 took longer than we thought.' They can make a similar chart for activities in science and PE, on which they estimate and then measure how long particular activities will take.

- **Activity Sheet 11** – To introduce the activity, show the children a chart in a diary showing sunrise and sunset times. Explain that the times are always written using 24-hour clock notation and that the times change every day throughout the year, depending on whether the days are lengthening or shortening. The children should be confident with writing 24-hour times. They could find out the current sunrise and sunset times and work out how much earlier or later than sunrise/sunset they get up/go to bed.

▶ **Clocks, Watches and Timers: Level 4**

- **Activity Sheet 12** – Ask the children to complete the puzzle in pairs. Ensure that they read the instructions carefully and notice that the starting time for both monkeys is 14:30. They will need pencils in two different colours. When they have finished, they could check their answers by turning the hands of a traditional mechanical clock. They could also convert the times for each monkey into 12-hour a.m. and p.m. times.

- **Activity Sheet 13** – Encourage the children to explain and record how they solve the problems. They could work in pairs. Questions could also be set about the cost of the day out, for example 'The entrance tickets cost £16.50 for adults and £10.50 for children. How much do the tickets cost altogether for Nick's parents, himself and his sister?' and 'Lunch costs £3.10 for each person. How much does it cost altogether?'

- **Activity Sheet 14** – The children will need to show their workings on another sheet of paper. Ensure that they know how to find the average lap time. You could ask more questions based on the activity, for example 'Graham completes four laps in 394 seconds. How much faster than Clare is he? What is his average lap time?'

Support

For Activity Sheet 11, change the times in parts c) and d) to make the calculation in part e) more straightforward. When writing when they get up and go to bed, suggest that the children round the times to the nearest 15 minutes.

Use Generic Sheet 2 (page 31) for practice in reading the time to the nearest minute. Working in pairs, the children should take turns to pick a card and find the matching time.

Challenge

After completing Activity Sheet 9, the children could work in groups to make a similar chart showing activities throughout the school day, using 24-hour clock notation.

For Activity Sheet 13, change the times in the questions to 24-hour times. Ask the children to write the answers as 24-hour times.

Plenary

Enlarge and use the cut-out cards from Generic Sheet 3 (page 32). Ask children to come to the front of the class and take one card each. They have to find their 'partners'. The rest of the class can give clues.

Display opportunity

Make a display entitled 'Time in everyday life'. Ask the children to look for examples of clocks, timers and timetables at school, in the home and in the local environment. These might include an alarm clock, an oven timer, a train timetable and a clock on a computer screen. They can collect or draw pictures to glue on to the display. Discuss which of the items normally use the 12-hour clock and which normally use the 24-hour clock. Label or sort the pictures accordingly.

Extra activities

Use Generic Sheet 3 (page 32) for practising matching 24-hour digital times, 12-hour digital times and times in words. Explain that the digital clocks all show 24-hour times. The children's task is to cut out the cards and match the equivalent times. They should read each time very carefully, and be aware that most of the cards will be in pairs, but some will be in groups of three.

The cards showing 24-hour times can also be used for the following activities: arranging in order; finding the number of minutes to the next hour; finding the number of hours and minutes to the next day; adding or subtracting a specified period of time (for example 'add 40 minutes' or 'subtract 80 minutes'. Extra cards could be made showing other 24-hour times.

Answers

Activity Sheet 11

1. a) 10 hrs 30 mins   b) 13 hrs 30 mins
   c) 07:05   d) 21:15   e) 9 hrs 50 mins

2. a) 15 hrs 50 mins   b) 8 hrs 10 mins
   c) 06:50   d) 21:40   e) 9 hrs 10 mins

Activity Sheet 12

Monkey A
14:30 15:25 16:20 17:15 18:10 19:05 20:00 20:55 21:50 22:45 23:40
Monkey B
14:30 14:05 13:40 13:15 12:50 12:25 12:00 11:35 11:10 10:45

Activity Sheet 13

1. 4:20 p.m.   2. 10:28 a.m.   3. 17 mins
4. 1:19 p.m.   5. 2:19 p.m.   6. 3:45 p.m.

Activity Sheet 14

1. Lap 3   2. Lap 4   3. 206.6 secs
4. 209.4 secs   5. 416 secs   6. 11.8 secs
7. 18.4 secs   8. 104 secs

Name_____

▶ Clocks – Activity Sheet 7

On time

Write the time in words to the nearest minute.

_____
_____

_____
_____

_____
_____

_____
_____

_____
_____

_____
_____

Write the time in words.

| 3:48 | 7:06 | 11:19 |

_____
_____

| 2:56 | 6:24 | 9:31 |

_____
_____

PHOTOCOPIABLE
© Hopscotch Educational Publishing 2002

Name_____   ▸ Clocks – Activity Sheet 8

Mystery phrase game

Cut out the cards. Place each a.m. or p.m. time beneath the matching 24-hour time.

Put the times in order. The letters in the circles will spell out two words.

21:55 (C)	13:23 (C)	00:51 (D)
02:43 (G)	01:23 (I)	11:22 (A)
18:11 (O)	22:11 (K)	12:51 (L)
15:09 (L)	09:55 (T)	06:11 (I)
2:43 a.m.	11:22 a.m.	1:23 p.m.
6:11 p.m.	9:55 a.m.	12:51 p.m.
10:11 p.m.	12:51 a.m.	6:11 a.m.
1:23 a.m.	9:55 p.m.	3:09 p.m.

PHOTOCOPIABLE

Name_____

▶ Clocks – Activity Sheet 9

Don't forget!

Read the notes in Gran's kitchen.

- 7:28 p.m. Video Animal Hospital
- 8:00 a.m. Feed Sooty
- 12:45 p.m. Go to post office
- 1:44 p.m. Watch Neighbours
- 9:59 p.m. Watch news
- 5:15 p.m. Feed Sooty
- 8:05 p.m. Ring Claire
- 10:13 a.m. Meet David off train

Write the activities in order on the notepad. Write the times in words, then using the 24-hour clock. One has been done for you.

Activity	Time in words	24-hour time
Feed Sooty	eight o'clock in the morning	08:00

PHOTOCOPIABLE
© Hopscotch Educational Publishing 2002

Name_____   ▸ Clocks – Activity Sheet 10

Estimating time

Estimate how long it will take to do each task. Write your estimates on the chart.

Use a timer to measure the actual time it takes. Complete the chart.

Estimate in seconds or minutes.

Task 1
Write the 8 times table (up to 10 x 8).

Task 2
Draw five rectangles accurately.

Task 3
Work out how many hours there are in one week.

Task 4
Find five facts about frogs and write them in a paragraph.

	Task 1	Task 2	Task 3	Task 4
Estimated time				
Actual time				

Work out the difference between the estimated time and the actual time.

Task 1 _____   Task 2 _____

Task 3 _____   Task 4 _____

PHOTOCOPIABLE
© Hopscotch Educational Publishing 2002

Name_____   ▸ Clocks Activity Sheet 11

Night and day

1. In October, the sun rises at 07:30 and sets at 18:00.
   a) For how long is the day light? _____
   b) For how long is the day dark? _____
   c) Rachel gets up 25 minutes before sunrise. Write this as a 24-hour time. _____
   d) She goes to bed 3 hours and 15 minutes after sunset. Write this as a 24-hour time. _____
   e) For how long does Rachel sleep each night? _____

2. In May, the sun rises at 05:00 and sets at 20:50.
   a) For how long is the day light? _____
   b) For how long is the day dark? _____
   c) Joshua gets up 1 hour and 50 minutes after sunrise. Write this as a 24-hour time. _____
   d) He goes to bed 50 minutes after sunset. Write this as a 24-hour time. _____
   e) For how long does Joshua sleep each night? _____

3. What time do you get up and go to bed? Write them as 24-hour times.
   I get up at _____. I go to bed at _____.

4. Work out how long you sleep each night. _____

Clocks – Activity Sheet 12

Monkey puzzle

Work with a partner. Find a path to the bananas for each monkey. Draw the paths in different colours.

Monkey A can move only to times that are 55 minutes later.

Monkey B can move only to times that are 25 minutes earlier.

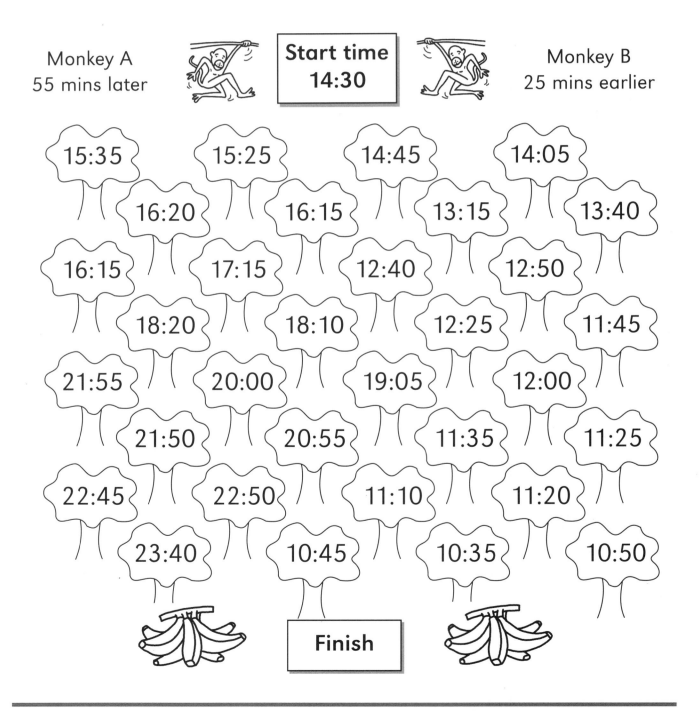

PHOTOCOPIABLE
© Hopscotch Educational Publishing 2002

Name_____   ▸ Clocks – Activity Sheet 13

Wet 'n' Wild

Solve these problems about
Nick's trip to a theme park.

1. Nick and his family arrived at the theme park at 9:50 a.m. They left $6\frac{1}{2}$ hours later. What time did they leave?

   _____

2. The trip on the cable car took 18 minutes. It finished at 10:46 a.m. What time did it start?

   _____

3. Nick got on the Log Flume at 11:06 a.m. He got off at 11:23 a.m. How long did it last?

   _____

4. He went for lunch at 12:35 p.m. He queued for 9 minutes. He took 35 minutes to eat his lunch. What time did he finish?

   _____

5. Nick got on the Pirate Ship at 1:55 p.m. He stayed on for three rides. Each ride took 8 minutes. What time did he get off?

   _____

6. The Aqua Show lasted for 85 minutes. It started at 2:20 p.m. What time did it finish?

   _____

Name _____ ▸ Clocks – Activity Sheet 14

Go-karting

Clare went go-karting. These are her times.

| Lap 1 | 109.2 secs | Lap 2 | 97.4 secs |
| Lap 3 | 95.5 secs | Lap 4 | 113.9 secs |

Answer the questions. For questions 3 to 8, give your answers in minutes and seconds.

1. Which was the fastest lap? _____

2. Which was the slowest lap? _____

3. How long did Lap 1 and Lap 2 take altogether?
_____

4. How long did Lap 3 and Lap 4 take altogether?
_____

5. How long did all four laps take?
_____

6. How much slower was Lap 1 than Lap 2?
_____

7. How much faster was Lap 3 than Lap 4?
_____

8. What was Clare's average lap time?
_____

PHOTOCOPIABLE
© Hopscotch Educational Publishing 2002

▶ Clocks, Watches and Timers: Level 5

▶ UNIT 1: CLOCKS, WATCHES AND TIMERS
LEVEL 5

🕒 Learning objectives

- To read any time from an analogue or digital clock, using the correct notation.
- To appreciate different times around the world.
- To have knowledge of local time, Greenwich Mean Time, British Summer Time and the International Date Line.

Key vocabulary

- analogue, digital, Greenwich Mean Time, British Summer Time, International Date Line

🕒 Resources

- classroom analogue clock
- digital clock
- traditional mechanical clocks
- globe • atlas
- world time map (see page 34)

🕒 Introduction

- Discuss with the class what the current time is in Britain and in another city such as New York (GMT –5 hours). Discuss why the time varies across the world, using a globe to model the movements of the Sun (for example if the Sun rises at 7:00 a.m. in London, it will still be dark in New York: there needs to be a time difference of five hours because the Sun rises approximately five hours later in New York than in London). Tell the children the time difference for other world cities, such as Helsinki (GMT +2 hours) and Beijing (GMT +8 hours) and ask them to work out what the current time is in these places.
- Introduce and explain the terms local time, Greenwich Mean Time (GMT) and International Date Line (IDL). Show the children a globe and point out the International Date Line (which approximately follows the 180° line of longitude). The children could search the Internet to find the history of Greenwich Mean Time.
- Discuss how we put the clocks forward in spring and back in autumn, and ask if the children know why we do this. Introduce the term British Summer Time (BST). Show how BST affects time differences.

🕒 Activities

- **Activity Sheet 15** – This activity can be used to introduce the concept of time differences within a smaller area, before moving on to looking at time across the world. Ask the children if any of them have been to the USA and, if so, whether they can remember by how much they had to adjust their watches. Discuss the map with the class and explain that the USA is split into four regions with different times, called time zones. Remind the children that Greenwich Mean Time (GMT) is the time in London. Demonstrate how to read the map.

- **Activity Sheet 16** – Before beginning the activity, show the children the location of Sydney on a globe and work out what the current time is there. (Note that around the start and end of British Summer Time there may be a time difference of +9 or +11 hours instead of +10. The children could research when people in Australia change their clocks for summer time.) The children will need to be confident in using 24-hour notation. Remind them that they need to subtract 10 hours and $5^1/_2$ hours, not add, in order to find the time in London and New Delhi. Ensure they realise that when it is early morning in Sydney, it is still the previous day in Europe and many other parts of the world.

- **Activity Sheet 17** – For this game, the children will need copies of the world map on Generic Sheet 5 (page 34). The game can be played in pairs or with three or four players. Encourage them to check each other's answers and to keep a tally of how many 'goals' each player has scored. They should keep each card they answer correctly and continue playing until all the cards are gone. They could play a variation of the game in which they say the time the match finishes (remind them how long a football match lasts including half-time).

▶ Clocks, Watches and Timers: Level 5

- **Activity Sheet 18** – Before beginning the activity, show the children the location of each city on a globe and ask them to work out the current time in each city. Explain that for question 7, Holly can phone at any time when both she and the person she is ringing are awake.

- **Activity Sheet 19** – Practise adding and subtracting periods of time by asking questions such as 'I put a stew in the oven at 15:48. It cooks for 75 minutes. What time do I take it out?' Talk through the notes on the activity sheet. The children could solve the problems in pairs. They could make a chart showing each item, what time it needs to start cooking and how long it takes.

Support

Show the children a map of Europe with the time zones marked on (GMT, GMT +1 and GMT +2). Demonstrate how to use the map to work out the time in any given European city. Ask them to say the current time in Paris, Lisbon, Vienna, Helsinki, Dublin, Athens and so on.

For Activity Sheet 19, change the notes to show how long each item takes to cook. Ask the children to work out what time Harry's dad needs to start cooking each item. This can be repeated for different serving times.

Challenge

Ask the children to research which other countries change their daylight times in the summer, using books, CD-ROMs and the Internet. They could also research the differences in daily routines around the world (for example shop opening times and siestas) and suggest reasons for the differences.

Plenary

Organise the children into groups of five or six. Each group 'lives' in a nominated country and needs to be aware of their time zone in relation to GMT. The teacher or a child 'goes travelling round the world' and wants to phone their friends. For example 'I am in Washington D.C. and it 3:30 p.m. local time. Can I phone my friend in Tokyo?' The responses will be 'We will be asleep/at school/eating breakfast' and so on.

Display opportunity

Display a large wall map of the world. Mark the time zones with lines and label them. Mark a number of major cities with pins. List the cities next to the map on a laminated piece of card or a wipe-clean board. At various times throughout the day, ask the children to come and write what the current time is in each of the cities.

Answers

Activity Sheet 15

1. a) 2 hrs   b) 3 hrs   c) 5 hrs
2. a) 8:45 a.m.   b) 5:45 a.m.   c) 7:45 a.m.
   d) 8:45 a.m.   e) 6:45 a.m.   f) 7:45 a.m.

Activity Sheet 16

Event	Time in UK	Time in New Delhi
100 m hurdles	08:55	14:25
100 m sprint	00:35	06:05
200 m sprint	07:15	12:45
400 m hurdles	02:25	07:55
4 x 100 m relay	09:20	14:50
4 x 400 m relay	01:00	06:30
800 m	00:05	05:35
Discus	03:20	08:50
Hammer	11:25	16:55
High jump	10:40	16:10
Javelin	23:45	05:15
Long jump	04:55	10:25
Pole vault	23:10	04:40
Shot put	09:45	15:15
Triple jump	05:50	11:20

Activity Sheet 18

1. No
2. No
3. 3:30 p.m.
4. 11:30 p.m.
5. One (Holly)
6. Two (Holly and Mark)
7. Examples of suitable times are: Mark – 8:00 p.m. Ming – 12:00 p.m. Jason – 10:00 a.m.

Activity Sheet 19

1. 17:35
2. 50 mins
3. 18:36
4. a) 17:55   b) 17:30   c) 17:05
5. 18:40
6. 2.5 kg roast beef   In at 11:15
   Roast potatoes   In at 12:10
   Roast parsnips   In at 12:30
   Yorks pudding   In at 12:45
   Sprouts   In at 13:09
   Broccoli   In at 13:11
   Gravy   Make at 13:12
   Sticky toffee pudding In at 13:10

Name_____   ▸ Clocks – Activity Sheet 15

USA time zones

Look at the map of the USA. It shows the difference between GMT and the time in the places on the map.

Remember, GMT means Greenwich Mean Time.

Answer the questions.

1   What is the time difference between:
    a) Phoenix and New York? _____
    b) Miami and Los Angeles? _____
    c) London and New York? _____

2   It is 1:45 p.m. in London. What time is it in:
    a) Atlanta? _____   b) San Francisco? _____
    c) Chicago? _____   d) Miami? _____
    e) Denver? _____   f) Minneapolis? _____

25

PHOTOCOPIABLE
© Hopscotch Educational Publishing 2002

Name_____   ▸ Clocks – Activity Sheet 16

Olympics on TV

The 2000 Olympics took place in Sydney, Australia. The time in Sydney is GMT +10 hours.

The chart shows the Athletics events for one day. Fill it in to show when you could watch the events in the UK and in New Delhi, in India, which is GMT +$5\frac{1}{2}$ hours.

Event	Time	Time in UK	Time in New Delhi
100 m hurdles	18:55		
100 m sprint	10:35		
200 m sprint	17:15		
400 m hurdles	12:25		
4 x 100 m relay	19:20		
4 x 400 m relay	11:00		
800 m	10:05		
Discus	13:20		
Hammer	21:25		
High jump	20:40		
Javelin	09:45		
Long jump	14:55		
Pole vault	09:10		
Shot put	19:45		
Triple jump	15:50		

PHOTOCOPIABLE
© Hopscotch Educational Publishing 2002

Name_____   ▸ Clocks – Activity Sheet 17

World Cup Final

The World Cup Final is played in Japan at 7:30 p.m. local time. The time in Japan is GMT +9 hours.

Cut out the cards. Take turns with a partner to pick a card.

Say what time each person starts watching the match in their country. Use the world map to help you.

For every correct answer, you score a goal. Who scores the most?

Marga watches the match in Rio de Janeiro, Brazil.	Steve watches the match in Washington D.C., USA.	Antonia watches the match in Rome, Italy.
Zac watches the match in Dublin, Republic of Ireland.	Sven watches the match in Stockholm, Sweden.	Ming watches the match in Nairobi, Kenya.
Jane watches the match in Cape Town, South Africa.	Hasan watches the match in Cairo, Egypt.	Reuben watches the match in Madrid, Spain.
Tony watches the match in Lagos, Nigeria.	Zahir watches the match in Islamabad, Pakistan.	Fran watches the match in Madrid, Spain.
Matt watches the match in Canberra, Australia.	Prakash watches the match in London, UK.	Ellen watches the match in Madrid, Spain.
Nikos watches the match in Athens, Greece.	Chandra watches the match in New Delhi, India.	Juan watches the match in Mexico City, Mexico.

PHOTOCOPIABLE
© Hopscotch Educational Publishing 2002

Name_____   ▸ Clocks – Activity Sheet 18

Global pen-pals

Four children from different countries are pen-pals.

 Holly
Leeds, UK
GMT

 Mark
Vancouver,
Canada
GMT –8

 Ming
Shanghai,
China
GMT +8

 Jason
Melbourne,
Australia
GMT +10

They all have the same daily routine.

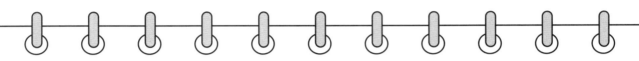

Get up 7:30 a.m.   Arrive at school 8:45 a.m.
Leave school 3:45 p.m.   Go to bed 9:30 p.m.

Answer the questions.

1   Is Jason asleep when Ming goes to bed? _____

2   Is Mark asleep when Holly goes to bed? _____

3   What time is it with Holly when Mark gets up? _____

4   What time is it with Jason when Ming goes to bed? _____

5   At 3:30 p.m. GMT, how many children are at school? _____

6   At 7:00 a.m. GMT, how many children are in bed? _____

7   Holly wants to phone Mark, Ming and Jason on Sunday.
    Suggest suitable times (GMT).
    a) Phone Mark at _____.
    b) Phone Ming at _____.
    c) Phone Jason at _____.

PHOTOCOPIABLE
© Hopscotch Educational Publishing 2002

Name _____   ▸ Clocks – Activity Sheet 19

Dad's dinner

Harry's dad is cooking a roast dinner. Read his notes.

Roast beef	Cook for 50 mins for every kg	
Roast potatoes	Need 70 mins	
Roast parsnips	In at 17:55	Serve at 18:45
Yorks pudding	Cook for 35 mins	
Sprouts	In at 18:34	
Broccoli	Steam for 9 mins	
Gravy	Make at 18:37	
Sticky toffee pud.	Serve at 19:35. Takes 55 mins.	

Answer the questions.

1 What time should the potatoes go in the oven?
   _____

2 How long do the parsnips take? _____

3 What time should the broccoli go in? _____

4 What time should the beef go in the oven if it weighs:
   a) 1 kg? _____ b) 1.5 kg? _____ c) 2 kg? _____

5 What time should the sticky toffee pudding go in? _____

6 If the meal needs to be served at 13:20, at what time does each thing need to be done?

2.5 kg roast beef	In at _____		Sprouts	In at _____
Roast potatoes	In at _____		Broccoli	In at _____
Roast parsnips	In at _____		Gravy	Make at _____
Yorks pudding	In at _____		Sticky toffee pudding	In at _____ Serve at 14:05

PHOTOCOPIABLE
© Hopscotch Educational Publishing 2002

Name_____   ▶ Clocks – Generic Sheet 1

Time cards

5:05	4:45	6:35	1:50
9:55	4:55	10:40	3:05
7:35	12:10	8:25	11:15

PHOTOCOPIABLE
© Hopscotch Educational Publishing 2002

Name_____   ▸ Clocks – Generic Sheet 2

Time cards

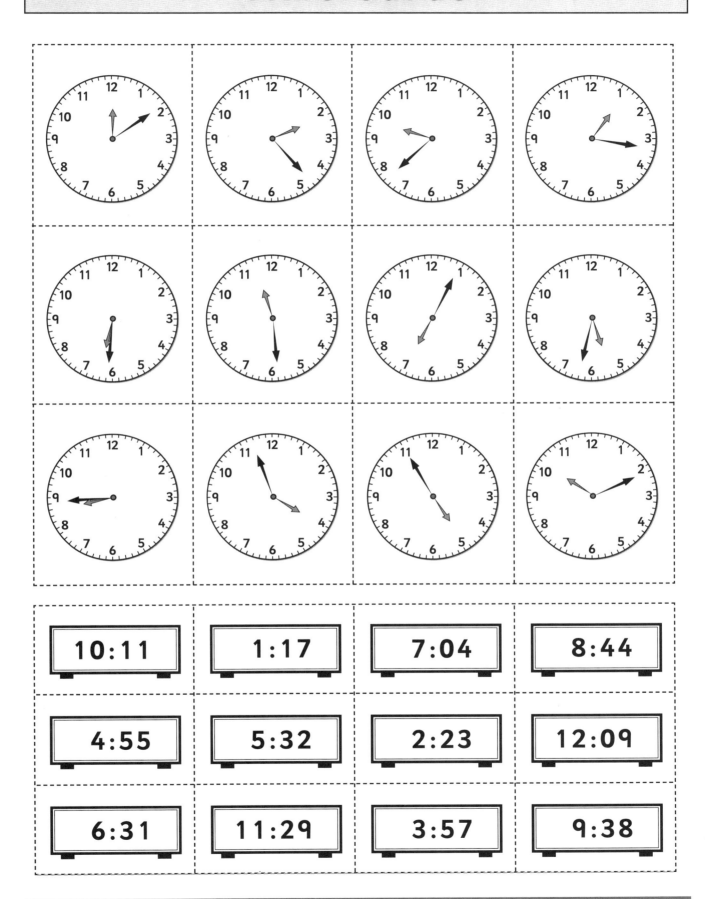

Time cards

00:04	11:56	06:15	18:45
19:36	04:12	12:04	13:28

1:28 p.m.	6:45 p.m.	12:04 a.m.	12:04 p.m.
6:15 p.m.	1:28 a.m.	7:36 p.m.	6:36 p.m.

12 minutes past 4 in the morning	4 minutes past midnight	quarter to 7 in the evening	4 minutes to midday
quarter past 6 in the evening	28 minutes past 1 in the morning	quarter past 6 in the morning	24 minutes to 7 in the evening

Name_____   ▸ Clocks – Generic Sheet 4

Analogue and digital

Analogue   Digital   Words

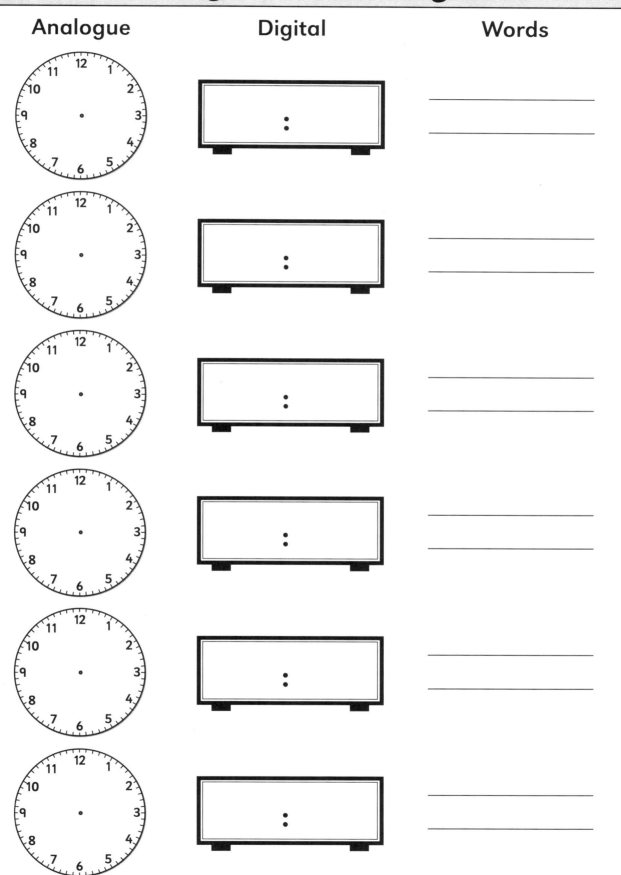

PHOTOCOPIABLE
© Hopscotch Educational Publishing 2002

Name_____   ▸ Clocks – Generic Sheet 5

World map

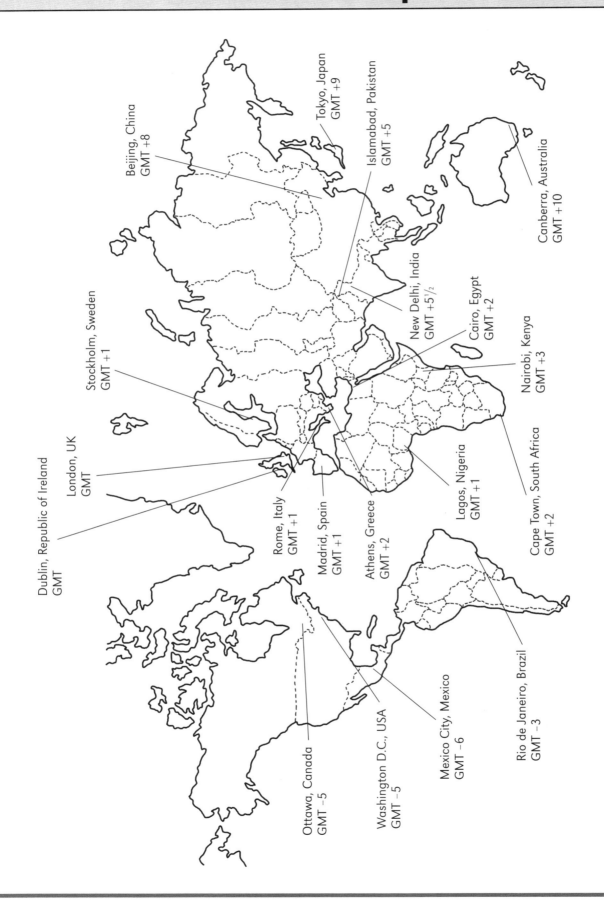

PHOTOCOPIABLE
© Hopscotch Educational Publishing 2002

Calendars and Diaries: Level 3

UNIT 2: CALENDARS AND DIARIES
LEVEL 3

Learning objectives

- To use units of time and know the relationships between them (second, minute, hour, day, week, month, year).
- To use a calendar.
- To solve problems involving time.

Key vocabulary

- day, week, fortnight, month, year, weekend, calendar, date

Resources

- copies of this year's calendar
- a range of diaries
- an enlarged calendar showing the current month, or an enlarged copy of Generic Sheet 3 (page 57), filled in for the current month

Introduction

- Revise the key vocabulary and ensure that the children are familiar with equivalent periods of time, for example 1 year = 365 days or 52 weeks or 12 months; 1 week = 7 days; 1 day = 24 hours; 1 hour = 60 minutes; 1 minute = 60 seconds. Introduce and explain the term 'century'.

- Display the current month from this year's calendar (or use Generic Sheet 3, page 57, enlarged to A3 size) on which you have written some events, such as parents' evening, half term, sports activities and so on. Ask the children questions about the events, such as 'On what day is the parents' evening?', 'What date is it?' and 'What date is the start of half term?' Then invite children to come and fill in other school events or activities on the calendar.

- Discuss the different ways of writing the date, for example 14 February 2002, February 14, 2002, 14th February 2002, 14.02.02, 14/2/02.

Activities

- **Activity Sheet 1** – Use this game to reinforce the relationships between units of time. The children should play in pairs (pair weaker readers with fluent ones). Each pair will need one copy of the sheet. Explain that for some of the cards both children will be able to cross out a square, but for others, neither of them will. They could record their answers on a separate piece of paper, for example '1 year = 365 days'. Encourage them to check each other's answers and ask them to write in pencil. After playing the game, they can rub out the crosses, swap grids, shuffle the cards and play again.

- **Activity Sheet 2** – Before beginning the activity, show the children a calendar of the current month and discuss how the days and dates are arranged. Revise how to write the date correctly, both in words and in the numerical form (they could practise writing their own date of birth and the date of their birthday this year). For questions 5 and 6, explain that they should count on from one date to the next (not including the first date in their count).

- **Activity Sheet 3** – The children can work on this activity in pairs or small groups. Each group will need this year's calendar or diary, showing the dates of the events listed on the page. Many diaries have lists of notable dates at the front or back which can be used to find the date. Explain that most of these dates change from year to year (the children could find out which ones do not change). They could enter the dates on a yearly planner by writing the date and the name of the event on the correct month (for example on the month of February they write '14 Valentine's Day'). Use the yearly planner on Generic Sheet 2, page 56. For the second part of the activity, provide a calendar of the academic year with the school term dates marked on. Discuss how the academic year is different from the calendar year, and why.

- **Activity Sheet 4** – Read the notes with the children before they begin the activity. Each child will need a copy of Generic Sheet 5 (page 59) for recording the appointments. Show them

▶ Calendars and Diaries: Level 3

how to fill in the dates across the top of the diary page, for example 'Monday 19 May', 'Tuesday 20 May' and so on. Suggest that they show periods of time on the diary by drawing an arrow (they write 'Cleaner' alongside 1:00 and draw an arrow from there ending at 3:00). They could draw arrows to help them answer the questions relating to duration.

Support

The children could work in pairs on Activity Sheet 1, focusing on one grid at a time instead of playing it as a game. They can go through the cards together, writing the equivalent time on the back of each card as they find it.

Give the children a copy of Generic Sheet 3 (page 57) and ask them to write the name of this month at the top. Ask them to find today's date on the planner and fill in the correct day of the week. They can then use this to complete the days of the week on the rest of the planner. Write a set of events and their dates for the children to write in the notes column. Questions could be asked about the days of the week on which the events fall.

Challenge

Give the children copies of Generic Sheet 4 (page 58) and some recent newspapers or leaflets containing information on local events in the near future. Ask them to fill in the planner with the correct dates for this week and next week, and then find events to enter on the planner. They could also use the Internet for research (give them the addresses of websites with 'What's on' information for your local area).

Plenary

Enlarge Generic Sheet 5 (page 59) and fill in some appointments. Make some statements about the timings shown on the diary and ask the children to say whether each one is true or false. They could respond by giving thumbs up for true and thumbs down for false.

Display opportunity

Ask the children to collect adverts and information about local events from newspapers and the Internet. Make a display showing the events in chronological order. Add to the display frequently.

Extra activities

Play a dice game using Generic Sheet 1 (page 55) to practise using calendars and writing the date. Group the children into fours and give each group two copies of the sheet and this year's calendar. Ask them to write the names of any six months on the faces of one dice and any numbers between 1 and 28 on the faces of the other. They should then cut out each template, fold it into a cube along the lines, spread glue on the tabs and fix them to the inside of the adjacent faces of the cube. Taking it in turns, each child rolls both dice to give a date. He or she should then find that date on the calendar and write down the day and date correctly. The children can check each other's answers and score points when they are correct.

Answers

Activity Sheet 2

1. Wednesday
2. Tuesday 1/10/02
3. Friday
4. a) 10/10/02
   b) 5/10/02
   c) 4/10/02
   d) 12/10/02 and 13/10/02
5. 3
6. 5

Activity Sheet 4

1. 25 mins
2. 4:15 p.m.
3. 3 hrs 30 mins
4. 2:50 p.m.
5. £13.00

Name _____   ▸ Calendars – Activity Sheet 1

Bingo!

Play this game with a friend. Each write your name on a grid.

Cut out the cards at the bottom of the page. Place them in a pile face down.

With your partner, turn over the cards one by one. If you can find a time on your grid that is the same as the card, cross it out.

Who can cross out all their numbers first?

Name _____   Name _____

52 weeks	35 days	6 months
120 seconds	2 weeks	60 minutes
48 hours	a century	3600 seconds

300 minutes	14 days	24 hours
30 seconds	365 days	6 weeks
24 months	120 minutes	520 weeks

1 year	3 years	2 hours	5 hours
10 years	2 days	half a year	2 minutes
100 years	half a minute	2 years	1 hour
42 days	5 weeks	a fortnight	1 day

PHOTOCOPIABLE
© Hopscotch Educational Publishing 2002

Chris's calendar

This is part of Chris's calendar. Answer the questions.

October 2002

M	T	W	T	F	S	S
	1 Play tennis	2 Piano lesson	3	4 Go to cinema	5 Football match	6
7 Ed round for tea	8	9 Piano lesson	10 Sam's party	11	12 Visit Gran and Grandad	13

1 On what day of the week does Chris have piano lessons?
  _____

2 What day and date is the first day of the month?
  _____

3 What day of the week is 11/10/02? _____

4 Write the dates when Chris:
   a) goes to a party _____
   b) goes to a football match _____
   c) goes to the cinema _____
   d) visits his grandparents _____

5 How many days from 2/10/02 to 5/10/02? _____

6 How many days from 8/10/02 to 13/10/02? _____

Name_____   ▸ Calendars – Activity Sheet 3

Dates to remember

Find out when these events happen this year. Use a calendar or diary. Write the correct day and date.

Valentine's Day _____

St David's Day _____

Eid-ul-Fitr _____

Shrove Tuesday _____

the shortest day _____

the longest day _____

Good Friday _____

Divali _____

your birthday _____

Remembrance Sunday _____

Rosh Hashanah (Jewish New Year) _____

Find out your school term dates for this school year. Write the days and dates.

Autumn term starts _____

ends _____

Spring term starts _____

ends _____

Summer term starts _____

ends _____

PHOTOCOPIABLE
© Hopscotch Educational Publishing 2002

Name_____   ▸ Calendars – Activity Sheet 4

Things to do

Mr Gray has had a busy week. Read his notes about his appointments.

Dentist - Mon 19 May 9:00

Rags to vet - 22 May 2:30

Car repair Tuesday 11 a.m.

Cleaner - Friday 23rd 1:00-3:00

Doctor - Thurs 10:30

Estate agent - Wed 21st 4 p.m.

Haircut - Monday 10:30 a.m.

Joiner - 20th May 1:30

Plumber - Friday 8 a.m.

Optician - 19th May 5 p.m.

Job interview - Tuesday 20th 3:00

Write the dates on a 'One week' diary page. Write each appointment on the correct day and time.

Answer the questions.

1. Mr Gray left the hairdresser's at 10:55 a.m. How long did his haircut take? _____

2. Mr Gray's job interview took 75 minutes. What time did it finish?
_____

3. The car was ready at 2:30 p.m. For how long was it at the garage?
_____

4. The joiner stayed for 1 hour and 20 minutes. What time did he leave?
_____

5. The cleaner charges £6.50 per hour. How much did Mr Gray pay her?
_____

PHOTOCOPIABLE
© Hopscotch Educational Publishing 2002

▶ Calendars and Diaries: Level 4

▶ UNIT 2: CALENDARS AND DIARIES
LEVEL 4

Learning objectives

- To use this year's calendar.
- To use a.m. and p.m. and the notation 9:53.
- To use 24-hour clock notation, such as 19:53.
- To solve problems involving time.

Key vocabulary

- leap year, millennium, calendar, date of birth

Resources

- copies of this year's calendar
- a range of enlarged calendars, planners and diary pages (see Generic Sheets 2–6, pages 56–60)

Introduction

- Use an enlarged calendar to revise finding particular dates. Show the children how to find the number of days or the number of weeks between two dates in answer to questions such as 'How many days from 19 January to 3 February?' and 'How many weeks from 25 May to 15 June?'

- Demonstrate how to fill in dates and record events on a yearly, monthly and fortnightly planner, using enlarged copies of Generic Sheets 2–4 (pages 56–58). Then show how to record appointments next to particular times, using enlarged copies of Generic Sheets 5 and 6 (pages 59–60). Generic Sheet 5 could be adapted to show 24-hour times instead of 12-hour ones. Discuss the advantages and disadvantages of the different types of planner, and talk about what situations each one is useful for.

- Discuss abbreviations of the months of the year.

Activities

- **Activity Sheet 5** – Read the poem with the children and encourage them to learn it a line at a time, working in pairs and testing each other. Explain the term 'leap year' and discuss when the last one was and when the next one will be (referring to calendars of this year and previous years). Ask the children how many days there are in a leap year. Remind them that they must not look at the poem while they are completing the crossword. Once they have finished, they can uncover the poem and check their crossword answers are correct.

- **Activity Sheet 6** – Revise how many years there are in a leap year, a decade, a century and a millennium. Ask the children to play the game in pairs (pair weaker readers with fluent ones). Instead of putting the cards in a line, they could place them in a circle so that the last card joins up with the first one in a continuous loop.

- **Activity Sheet 7** – The children will need diaries or copies of this year's calendar. Discuss that the answers to questions 1 and 2 will vary from one year to the next, but that the answers to questions 3 and 4 are the same for all years (unless they are affected by leap years). For question 3, explain that they should count on from one date to the next (not including the first date in their count).

- **Activity Sheet 8** – The children will need copies of this year's calendar. Read the notices together and discuss them. Point out the abbreviation 'incl.' and explain what it means. Ask which of the other time periods will be inclusive, for example whether they think the football tournament will start on 22 July and finish on 30 July; if so, the dates at both ends of the period should be counted in question 1.

- **Activity Sheet 9** – The children will need copies of this year's calendar. Read the notes with the children and explain that home matches can be marked on the fixture list with 'H' and away matches with 'A'. Show them how to record the matches by writing the date first, then the team, then H or A, for example under October '13 Man Utd A'. Explain that the notes are not written in chronological order, so the children will need to think carefully about where to write each fixture on the list so that the finished list is in chronological order.

▶ Calendars and Diaries: Level 4

- **Activity Sheet 10** – For the first part of this activity, you could ask the children to write their date of birth on the sheet and then to come out in turn and write it on the board. Once all of them have done this, divide the class into groups of approximately 15 and ask them to fill in the table with the dates of birth of the other children in their group. For question 4 they will need copies of this year's calendar and for question 5 they will need blank yearly planners (see Generic Sheet 2, page 56). Children who attempt question 6 will need squared paper on which to draw the bar chart. As a further extension, they could choose a month in which several children have their birthday and draw a timeline of the month, marking the names next to the correct days.

- **Activity Sheet 11** – The children will need to be familiar with both the 12-hour and 24-hour clock for this activity. For questions 4 and 5 they will need to show their workings on a separate sheet of paper. Encourage them to explain to a partner the methods they used to solve the problems. During the plenary, compare the methods the children used.

Support

Ask the children to bring in a fixture list for their favourite sports team (or they could find one on the Internet). Give them copies of Generic Sheet 2 (page 56) and ask them to record the day and date of each match on the yearly planner.

Challenge

After completing Activity Sheet 9, the children could work out how long Rob will spend watching football if he goes to all the home matches on the fixture list (remind them that a football match lasts for 90 minutes). You could also ask them to work out how long he will spend travelling if it takes him 20 minutes to travel to the home ground.

Enlarge Generic Sheet 2 (page 56) and ask the children to research dates on the Internet and fill them in on the planner. Give them a topic to research, for example festivals across a range of religions; festivals and holidays in a particular country; or school term dates for different countries (such as France, Japan, Australia, USA).

The children could also create a planner for their own academic year on a computer, blocking in the holidays and training days.

Plenary

Ask the children the different methods they used to calculate the time intervals in questions 4 and 5 on Activity Sheet 11. Compare these methods and discuss the advantages and disadvantages of each method. Encourage the children to choose the method that they find the easiest.

Display opportunity

Photocopy or create a large yearly planner to display in the classroom. Mark on holidays and important events in the school year. Ask the children questions for them to answer using the planner, such as 'How many days until half term?', 'How many weeks until the start of the summer holidays?' and 'How many months and days until your birthday?'

Answers

Activity Sheet 7

1. and 2. Answers will vary from year to year.
3. a) 14
   b) 20
   c) 16 or 17
   d) 17
4. a) 3
   b) 4
   c) 4
   d) 7

Activity Sheet 8

1. 9
2. 6 August
3. 18
4. 4
5. 23
6. Answers will vary from year to year.
7. Answers will vary from year to year.
8. 7 August

Activity Sheet 9

Answers will vary from year to year.

Activity Sheet 11

1. a) Mr Crowther
   b) Mr Haigh
   c) Miss Devlin
   d) Ms West
   e) Mrs O'Shea
2. a) 09:15
   b) 12:45
   c) 14:15
   d) 15:15
   e) 16:45
3. 45 mins
4. 5 hrs 15 mins
5. 3 hrs 45 mins

Name_____   ▸ Calendars – Activity Sheet 5

Poem of the year

Read and learn the poem.

> 30 days hath September,
> April, June and November.
> All the rest have 31,
> Except in February alone
> Which has but 28 days clear
> And 29 in each leap year.

Ask a friend to test you!

Cover the poem. Then complete the crossword puzzle.

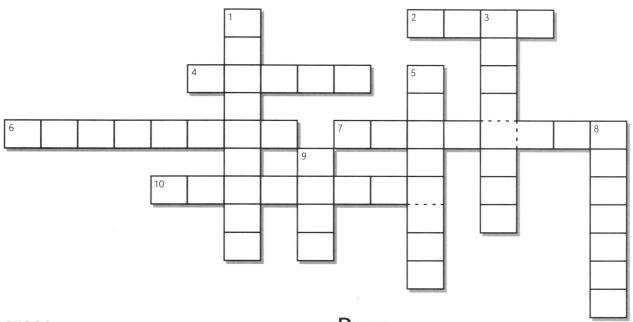

Across

2 A month with thirty-one days (4).
4 A month with thirty days (5).
6 A month with thirty days (8).
7 The total number of days in December and January (5-3).
10 The shortest month (8).

Down

1 A month with thirty days (9).
3 A year with 366 days (4, 4).
5 The total number of days in April and May (5-3).
8 A month with thirty-one days (7).
9 A month with thirty days (4).

PHOTOCOPIABLE
© Hopscotch Educational Publishing 2002

Name_____

▸ Calendars – Activity Sheet 6

A matter of time

Cut out the cards. Cut only along the dotted lines.

Pick a card and read the question.

Find the answer on another card. Place the answer next to the question.

Continue until all the cards are in a line. The answer to the last question should be on the first card.

26	How many days in a leap year?	400	How many seconds in 5 minutes?
56	How many years in 4 centuries?	360	How many weeks in half a year?
12	How many years in 9 decades?	600	How many weeks in 84 days?
90	How many centuries in 700 years?	366	How many years in half a millennium?
11	How many minutes in 10 hours?	300	How many months in 3 years?
104	How many days in 8 weeks?	7	How many minutes in 6 hours?
36	How many decades in 110 years?	500	How many weeks in 2 years?

PHOTOCOPIABLE
© Hopscotch Educational Publishing 2002

Name_____   ▸ Calendars – Activity Sheet 7

Use a calendar

Use this year's calendar to answer the questions.

1 What day of the week is:

   a) 3 April? _____   b) your birthday? _____

   c) 25 September? _____   d) 15 May? _____

   e) 31 December? _____   f) 18 July? _____

2 What date is the:

   a) first Monday in January? _____

   b) third Thursday in July? _____

   c) last Friday in October? _____

   d) second Sunday in February? _____

   e) last Saturday in June? _____

   f) first Wednesday in March? _____

3 Work out how many days:

   a) from 22 June to 6 July _____

   b) from 19 April to 9 May _____

   c) from 25 February to 13 March _____

   d) from 16 October to 2 November _____

4 Work out how many weeks:

   a) from 14 August to 4 September _____

   b) from 30 March to 27 April _____

   c) from 6 December to 3 January _____

   d) from 17 September to 5 November _____

45

PHOTOCOPIABLE
© Hopscotch Educational Publishing 2002

Name_____   ▸ **Calendars – Activity Sheet 8**

What's on?

Read the notices. Use a calendar to help you answer the questions.

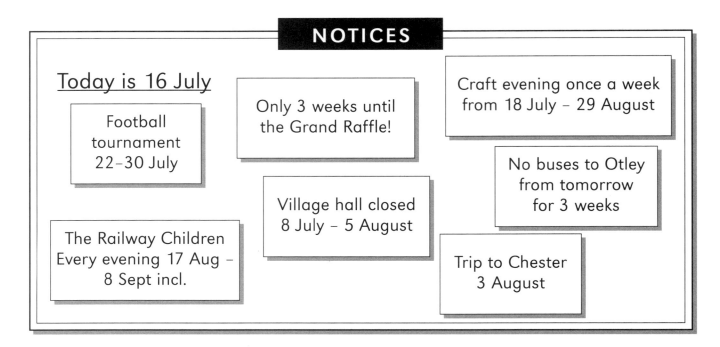

1 For how many days does the football tournament last? _____

2 What date is the Grand Raffle? _____

3 How many days until the trip to Chester? _____

4 For how many weeks is the village hall closed? _____

5 How many performances of **The Railway Children** are there? _____

6 On what day are the craft evenings held? _____

7 Write the dates of all the craft evenings.

   _____

   _____

8 On what date do the buses to Otley re-start? _____

PHOTOCOPIABLE
© Hopscotch Educational Publishing 2002

Name_____   ▸ Calendars – Activity Sheet 9

Football fixtures

Rob has made notes about his football team's matches this season. Read the notes. Using this year's calendar, write the dates on the fixtures list.

Man Utd away second Sunday in Oct.

Arsenal away last Saturday in Sept. West Ham home Saturday before that.

Away to Juventus last Wednesday in Oct, home leg 2 weeks later.

Everton away first Monday in Sept, then Newcastle home the following Saturday.

Chelsea away first Sunday in Nov, and Leeds home the following Saturday.

Aston Villa home first Saturday in Oct. Leicester home 2 weeks after that.

Sunderland home last Sunday in Nov.

FIXTURES

September	October	November

PHOTOCOPIABLE
© Hopscotch Educational Publishing 2002

Name_____   ▶ Calendars – Activity Sheet 10

Dates of birth

Write your date of birth.

_____

Find out the dates of birth of
14 other children in your class.

Name	Date of birth	Name	Date of birth

Answer the questions.

1   Who is the oldest? _____

2   Who is the youngest? _____

3   How many children have their birthdays:
    a) in April? _____ b) in June? _____
    c) in December? _____

4   Look at a calendar for this year. How many children have their birthdays:
    a) on a Monday? _____ b) on a Wednesday? _____
    c) on a Thursday? _____ d) at the weekend? _____

5   Fill in the birthdays on a yearly planner.

6   Draw a bar chart to show how many children have their birthdays in each month of the year.

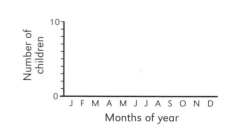

PHOTOCOPIABLE
© Hopscotch Educational Publishing 2002

Name_____   ▸ **Calendars – Activity Sheet 11**

Interview day

The headteacher, Mrs Sharp, has a busy day interviewing new teachers. Read her diary page.

8:00	
8:30	Ms West
9:00	
9:30	Mr Price
10:00	
10:30	
11:00	Mrs Day
11:30	
12:00	Miss Devlin
12:30	
1:00	
1:30	Mrs O'Shea
2:00	
2:30	Mr Crowther
3:00	
3:30	
4:00	Mr Haigh
4:30	
5:00	

Each interview lasts for 45 minutes. Answer the questions.

1. Who is with Mrs Sharp at these times?
   a) 2:54 p.m. _____
   b) 16:25 _____
   c) 12:09 p.m. _____
   d) 09:10 _____
   e) 13:48 _____

2. At what time do these people finish their interviews? Use the 24-hour clock.
   a) Ms West _____
   b) Miss Devlin _____
   c) Mrs O'Shea _____
   d) Mr Crowther _____
   e) Mr Haigh _____

3. How long does Mrs Sharp have for her lunch break?
   _____

4. How long does Mrs Sharp spend in interviews altogether?
   _____

5. How much time does Mrs Sharp have free between 8:00 a.m. and 5:00 p.m.? _____

PHOTOCOPIABLE
© Hopscotch Educational Publishing 2002

Calendars and Diaries: Level 5

UNIT 2: CALENDARS AND DIARIES
LEVEL 5

Learning objectives

- To use this year's calendar.
- To solve problems involving time.

Key vocabulary

- leap year, millennium, calendar

Resources

- copies of this year's calendar
- a range of enlarged calendars, planners and diary pages (see Generic Sheets 4–6, pages 58–60)

Introduction

- Revise the key vocabulary and the relationships between units of time. Show the children a variety of diaries in different formats and discuss what each format is useful for, for example appointments throughout the day, activities throughout the week or for recording personal thoughts and notes. Show them examples of filled-in diary pages with times recorded. Ask questions about the duration of activities in the diary.

Activities

- **Activity Sheet 12** – Revise how many years there are in a leap year, a decade, a century and a millennium. Encourage the children to read each question carefully to ensure they understand exactly what is being asked. They could use calculators to work out some of the more difficult multiplications. When they have written the answers, they can compare them with a partner and discuss (and correct if necessary) any answers which differ. They could work in pairs to find the numbers in the grid.

- **Activity Sheet 13** – Before beginning the activity, ask the children what activities they do in a typical day and remind them there are 24 hours in a day. Write their ideas on the board and ask if they can think of ways of grouping the activities, for example breakfast and lunch can be grouped under a heading 'mealtimes', and netball practice and computer games can be grouped under 'sport/hobbies'. Give the children the activity sheet along with a copy of Generic Sheet 6 (page 60). Demonstrate how to colour in blocks of time to show how the time in each day is spent. Then show them how to total the amount of time for each activity. Remind them that there are 60 minutes in one hour, so they need to be careful when adding or multiplying amounts of time. If they move on to questions 3 and 4, they will each need another two copies of Generic Sheet 6.

- **Activity Sheet 14** – Show the children examples of real diaries in the formats shown on the chart, and copies of Generic Sheets 4–6 (pages 58–60), filled in with example activities and appointments. Discuss the advantages and disadvantages of each format. Also, discuss how to record tallies (groups of fives). The children can do the survey in groups of four or five. Ensure that they talk to several adults and several children for their survey. The results for the whole class can be compiled to determine which diary format is the most popular.

Support

In Activity Sheet 13, the children could work with fewer activity categories, for example playtime, watching TV and sport/hobbies could be merged into one group entitled leisure time.

Challenge

After completing Activity Sheet 13, the children could draw a bar chart to show how much time they spend on each activity per day or per week. They could also find the amounts of time as percentages and draw a pie chart. Ask them to make other calculations, such as how long they have spent asleep, or how long they have spent eating, in their whole life.

▶ Calendars and Diaries: Level 5

🕐 Plenary

Having found the most popular format for a diary (Activity Sheet 14), use the plenary time to explain how all the children will fill in this particular diary for their homework. It could be for one or two weeks. Discuss what type of appointments/activities could be recorded. At the completion of the homework, all the children could be consulted about the ease/difficulty of using this format.

🕐 Display opportunity

Compile the children's results for Activity Sheet 13 and find the mean amount of time (per day or per week) spent on each activity. Make a class bar chart for display. Colour the chart according to the colour code on the activity sheet and display a key beneath.

🕐 Extra activities

Use the template on Generic Sheet 1 (page 55) to make a dice for adding and subtracting periods of time. Write on the faces of the dice times to add or subtract, for example '+ 2 h 40 mins', '– 80 mins', '+ 105 mins' and so on. Then cut out the template, fold it into a cube along the lines, spread glue on the tabs and fix them to the inside of the adjacent faces of the cube. The children can play the game in groups. Each child picks a time (they could use the time cards on Clocks – Generic Sheet 3, page 32), then rolls the dice to find out how much to add or subtract, and says the new 24-hour time. They can score points for every correct answer.

🕐 Answers

Activity Sheet 12

weeks in 3 years 156

days in a leap year 366

months in 7 years 84

years in a quarter of a millennium 250

years in $4\frac{1}{2}$ decades 45

centuries in a millennium 10

seconds in half an hour 1800

days in 4 years 1461

decades in 9 centuries 90

weeks in a decade 520

days in a standard year 365

decades in half a millennium 50

months in 12 years 144

centuries in 2000 years 20

minutes in one day 1440

days in 26 weeks 182

weeks in half a century 2600

Number crunching

Write the answers in figures. Find and ring them in the grid.

weeks in 3 years _____

days in a leap year _____

months in 7 years _____

years in a quarter of a millennium _____

years in 4½ decades _____

centuries in a millennium _____

seconds in half an hour _____

days in 4 years _____

decades in 9 centuries _____

weeks in a decade _____

days in a standard year ___

decades in half a millennium _____

months in 12 years _____

centuries in 2000 years _____

minutes in one day _____

days in 26 weeks _____

weeks in half a century _____

4	9	7	1	4	1	1	0
4	3	0	8	3	0	9	8
1	1	1	2	8	0	6	4
4	5	0	5	6	2	2	1
8	6	6	3	1	6	6	4
9	7	3	6	5	2	0	6
1	5	9	7	2	5	0	1
0	1	4	4	0	0	8	1

The answers in the grid are all horizontal or vertical. Some go backwards!

Name_____   ▸ Calendars – Activity Sheet 13

Time well spent?

Think about your daily routine on a typical schoolday.

1. Fill in the 'One day' diary page to show how you spend your time. Colour in the time periods.

Sleeping	colour orange
Mealtimes	colour green
Travelling	colour blue
Lessons	colour yellow
Playtime	colour brown
Watching TV	colour purple
Sport/hobbies	colour red
Other	leave blank

Round everything to the nearest quarter of an hour.

2. Use your diary page to help you fill in the chart.

Multiply by 5!

Activity	Time spent per day	Time spent per school week (5 days)
Sleeping		
Mealtimes		
Travelling		
Lessons		
Playtime		
Watching TV		
Sport/hobbies		
Other		

3. Now fill in a diary page for Saturday and one for Sunday. Think about what you usually do at the weekends.

4. Calculate how much time you spend on each activity:
   a) in a 7-day week
   b) in 4 weeks
   c) in 1 year (52 weeks)

PHOTOCOPIABLE
© Hopscotch Educational Publishing 2002

Name_____   ▸ Calendars – Activity Sheet 14

Diary survey

Look at a variety of different types of diary. You are going to investigate which is the most popular.

Ask 10 people which diary format they prefer, and why. Fill in the tally chart and note down their reasons.

Diary format	Tally	Total	Advantages	Disadvantages
1 day = 1 page				
1 week = 1 page				
1 week = 2 pages				
2 weeks = 1 page				
Other formats (specify)				

Draw a bar chart to show your results.

PHOTOCOPIABLE
© Hopscotch Educational Publishing 2002

Name_____   ▸ Calendars – Generic Sheet 1

Dice template

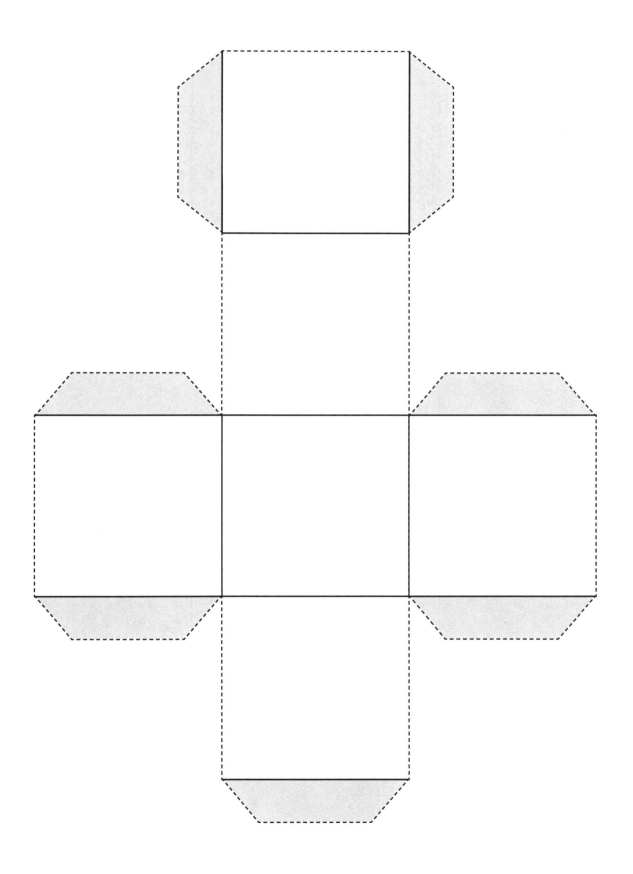

55

PHOTOCOPIABLE
© Hopscotch Educational Publishing 2002

Name_____ ▸ Calendars – Generic Sheet 2

Yearly planner

January	February	March
April	May	June
July	August	September
October	November	December

PHOTOCOPIABLE
© Hopscotch Educational Publishing 2002

Name_____   ▶ Calendars – Generic Sheet 3

Monthly planner

Date	Day	Notes
16		
17		
18		
19		
20		
21		
22		
23		
24		
25		
26		
27		
28		
29		
30		
31		

Month: _____

Date	Day	Notes
1		
2		
3		
4		
5		
6		
7		
8		
9		
10		
11		
12		
13		
14		
15		

PHOTOCOPIABLE
© Hopscotch Educational Publishing 2002

Name_____   ▸ Calendars – Generic Sheet 4

Fortnightly planner

Monday	Tuesday	Wednesday	Thursday	Friday	Saturday	Sunday
Monday	Tuesday	Wednesday	Thursday	Friday	Saturday	Sunday

PHOTOCOPIABLE
© Hopscotch Educational Publishing 2002

Name_____   ▸ Calendars – Generic Sheet 5

One week

Monday	Tuesday	Wednesday	Thursday	Friday
8:00	8:00	8:00	8:00	8:00
8:30	8:30	8:30	8:30	8:30
9:00	9:00	9:00	9:00	9:00
9:30	9:30	9:30	9:30	9:30
10:00	10:00	10:00	10:00	10:00
10:30	10:30	10:30	10:30	10:30
11:00	11:00	11:00	11:00	11:00
11:30	11:30	11:30	11:30	11:30
12:00	12:00	12:00	12:00	12:00
12:30	12:30	12:30	12:30	12:30
1:00	1:00	1:00	1:00	1:00
1:30	1:30	1:30	1:30	1:30
2:00	2:00	2:00	2:00	2:00
2:30	2:30	2:30	2:30	2:30
3:00	3:00	3:00	3:00	3:00
3:30	3:30	3:30	3:30	3:30
4:00	4:00	4:00	4:00	4:00
4:30	4:30	4:30	4:30	4:30
5:00	5:00	5:00	5:00	5:00
5:30	5:30	5:30	5:30	5:30

PHOTOCOPIABLE
© Hopscotch Educational Publishing 2002

Name_____ ▸ Calendars – Generic Sheet 6

One day

00:00	08:00	16:00
00:15	08:15	16:15
00:30	08:30	16:30
00:45	08:45	16:45
01:00	09:00	17:00
01:15	09:15	17:15
01:30	09:30	17:30
01:45	09:45	17:45
02:00	10:00	18:00
02:15	10:15	18:15
02:30	10:30	18:30
02:45	10:45	18:45
03:00	11:00	19:00
03:15	11:15	19:15
03:30	11:30	19:30
03:45	11:45	19:45
04:00	12:00	20:00
04:15	12:15	20:15
04:30	12:30	20:30
04:45	12:45	20:45
05:00	13:00	21:00
05:15	13:15	21:15
05:30	13:30	21:30
05:45	13:45	21:45
06:00	14:00	22:00
06:15	14:15	22:15
06:30	14:30	22:30
06:45	14:45	22:45
07:00	15:00	23:00
07:15	15:15	23:15
07:30	15:30	23:30
07:45	15:45	23:45

PHOTOCOPIABLE

© Hopscotch Educational Publishing 2002

▶ Timelines and Timetables: Level 3

▶ UNIT 3: TIMELINES AND TIMETABLES
LEVEL 3

Learning objectives

- To suggest suitable units to estimate or measure time.
- To solve problems involving time.

Key vocabulary

- day, week, fortnight, month, year, century, hour, minute, second

Resources

- classroom analogue clock
- digital clock
- traditional mechanical clocks
- timers or stopwatches

Introduction

- Introduce estimating time by helping the children to appreciate the length of one minute. Set a timer to one minute and let the time pass while the whole class sits in silence. You could ask the children to close their eyes and put their hand up when they think a minute has passed.

- Ask a question such as 'How long do you think it will take me to walk across the classroom and back?' Go through the key vocabulary (units of time) and invite the children first to select which unit is the most appropriate, then to write down their estimates. Using a stopwatch, time how long it takes you to walk across the room and back, and compare the estimates with the actual time. Repeat this for other practical situations. Then extend to estimating events or activities which take longer, for example travelling to the nearest large town.

Activities

- **Activity Sheet 1** – Before beginning the activity, ask the children to suggest events which take a short time and ones which take a long time. Write them on the board along with an appropriate selection of units of time, and ask the children to suggest which unit is suitable for which event. Emphasise that the children do not need to estimate how long each event on the sheet takes, but should simply choose a suitable unit of time. Explain that many questions have more than one possible answer, for example weeks or months would both be reasonable answers for planning a party.

- **Activity Sheet 2** – Use this sheet after the children have completed Activity Sheet 1. The pictures in the idea bank provide example answers. You could ask the children to give two suggestions for each period of time. For the second part of the activity, explain that they must choose which timeline to use for each period of time. Encourage them to first work out what the divisions on the timelines represent.

- **Activity Sheet 3** – Explain to the children that the activity is about a sponsored read, in which children take it in turns to read aloud from a novel so that the book is being read continuously for a whole morning. Ensure they understand that the start time of one child is the finish time of the previous child. Discuss what period of time each division on the timeline represents. This activity can be completed in pairs (pair weaker readers with fluent ones).

- **Activity Sheet 4** – The children will need to be confident with digital notation for this activity. They could use traditional mechanical clocks to help them work out the times, starting at 6:30 and turning the hands back by the required amount of time. Discuss what period of time each division on the timeline represents.

- **Activity Sheet 5** – Discuss the scoreboard and the timeline with the children, including what period of time each division on the timeline represents. Discuss mental strategies for working out the calculations and demonstrate how to count on and back along the timeline. The children could add Christian to the timeline once they have answered all the

Timelines and Timetables: Level 3

questions.

- **Activity Sheet 6** – This activity can link with work in history on the Tudors. Introduce Henry VIII and explain briefly what happened to each of his wives. Explain that this timeline shows important events in chronological order but that the line is not drawn to any particular scale. When finding the age of Henry VIII when he became king, the children may realise that this depends on whether he had already had his birthday in the year in question. However, for the purposes of this activity, they should simply find the difference between the two dates.

- **Activities Sheets 7 and 8** – Use these activity sheets together. Read the events in the speech bubble with the children and discuss what sort of events can be included on a timeline of someone's life, for example family events, personal achievements and special occasions. The children can make the timeline in pairs. Ask them to count the divisions on the timeline and work out what each division represents. For making the timeline of their own life, they will need a copy of Generic Sheet 4 (page 94). This sheet can be cut in half along the dotted lines and one half placed beneath the other to make a continuous timeline. The children may need help with labelling the years on the timeline. They should use Activity Sheet 8 as an example.

Support

For Activity Sheet 3, demonstrate how to make a simple table showing the name of each child and how long he or she read for. This can then be used to answer the questions.

For Activity Sheet 7, the children could simply write each date and event on the timeline next to the correct year (without joining it to the correct month). Provide ready-labelled timelines showing a relevant 10-year period for the children's own lives.

Challenge

After the children have completed Activity Sheet 4, ask them to draw a table showing what time each food needs to go in the oven if the party starts at 12:10 p.m.

As an extension to Activity Sheet 6, the children could make their own timeline showing all the Tudor monarchs, using Generic Sheet 5 (page 95). They will need two copies of the sheet (suggest that they begin the timeline at 1450 and end at 1650). The sheet can be cut in half along the dotted lines and one half placed beneath the other to make a continuous timeline. They can also research and add to the timeline other important events in the Tudor period, such as explorations.

Plenary

Enlarge Generic Sheet 4 (page 94) and label it to show the school day (8:30 a.m. – 4:30 p.m.). Laminate the sheet before the lesson. During the plenary, invite children to come to the front and mark on activities for that day. Discuss the length of time represented by each division on the timeline and talk about how long each activity lasts. This exercise can be repeated by different children at the beginning of each day, during register time.

Display opportunity

Make a large chart with units of time as headings: seconds, minutes, hours, days, weeks, months, years. Invite the children to write suitable events or activities under the headings, along with an estimate of how long each one takes. Where possible, check the actual time the activities take and add this to the chart.

Answers

Activity Sheet 1

1. minutes	2. hours
3. days or weeks	4. years
5. hours	6. minutes
7. days or weeks	8. seconds
9. years	10. seconds
11. weeks or months	12. months or years

Activity Sheet 3

1. 25 mins	2. 25 mins
3. 30 mins	4. Callum
5. Ben and Sue	6. 50 mins
7. 1 hr 20 mins	8. 2 hrs 50 mins

Activity Sheet 5

1. a) 5 secs	b) 12 secs	c) 30 secs
2. a) 7 secs	b) 18 secs	c) 25 secs
3. a) 11 secs	b) 16 secs	c) 23 secs
d) 34 secs	e) 41 secs	
4. a) 22 secs	b) 2nd	

Activity Sheet 6

1. 56	2. 38	3. 18
4. Catherine Howard	5. 4	
6. 24	7. 6	

Choose a unit

Dr Daze wants to show on a timeline how long each thing takes. Suggest which unit of time she should use.

1 baking a cake
   _____

2 time spent asleep last night
   _____

3 time to the end of the month
   _____

4 learning to speak French
   _____

5 a visit to a museum
   _____

6 having lunch
   _____

7 a holiday in France
   _____

8 doing up a tie
   _____

9 growing a tree
   _____

10 pouring a drink
   _____

11 planning a party
   _____

12 writing a book
   _____

Name_____   ▸ Timelines – Activity Sheet 2

Time teasers

For each question, write something that might take that amount of time to do.

1 10 minutes _____
   _____

2 4 weeks _____
   _____

3 2 hours _____
   _____

4 1 year _____
   _____

5 20 minutes _____
   _____

6 20 seconds _____
   _____

Idea bank

Mark each time with a cross on one of these timelines.

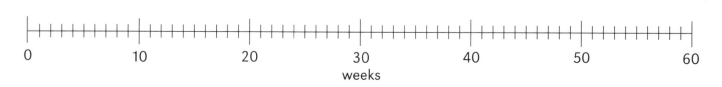

PHOTOCOPIABLE
© Hopscotch Educational Publishing 2002

Name_____   ▸ Timelines – Activity Sheet 3

Sponsored read

Class 3M did a sponsored read. Rosie started reading at 9:10 a.m. Her classmates took over one at a time, with no breaks in between.

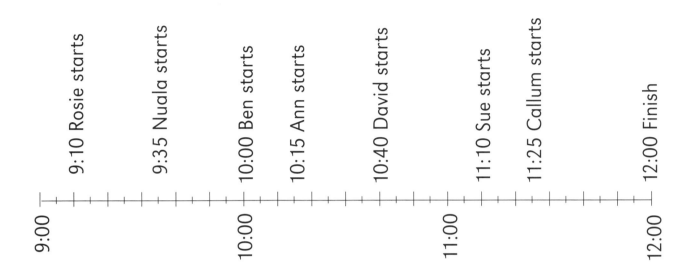

Answer the questions.

1   For how long did Rosie read? _____

2   For how long did Ann read? _____

3   For how long did David read? _____

4   Who read for the longest time? _____

5   Who read for the shortest time? _____
    and _____

6   For how long did Rosie and Nuala read altogether?
    _____

7   For how long did David, Sue and Callum read altogether?
    _____

8   For how long did all the children read altogether?
    _____

PHOTOCOPIABLE
© Hopscotch Educational Publishing 2002

Name_____   ▸ Timelines – Activity Sheet 4

Party food

Read the cooking instructions on the party food.

The party begins at 6:30 p.m. Write on each food when to put it in the oven.

Join each food to the correct place on the timeline.

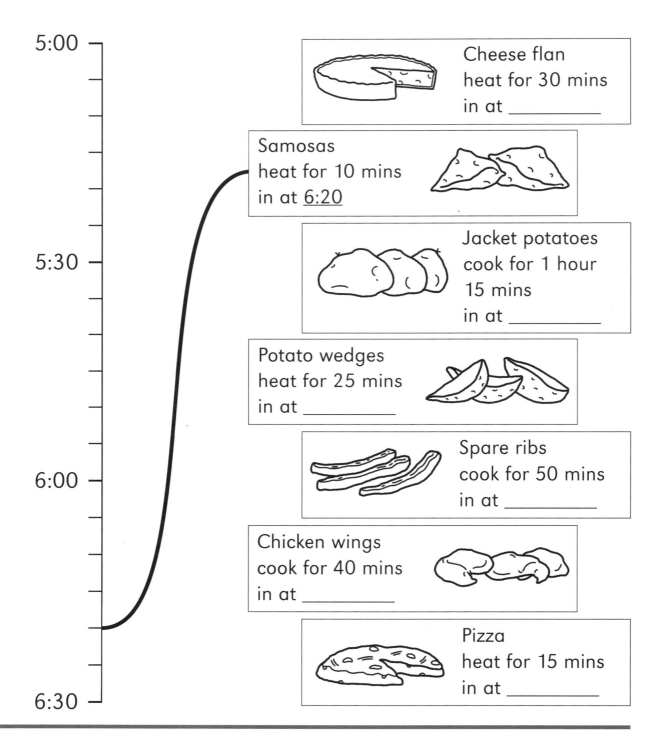

PHOTOCOPIABLE
© Hopscotch Educational Publishing 2002

Name_____   ▸ Timelines – Activity Sheet 5

Game scores

These are the winning times on a computer game scoreboard.

		Time			Time
1st	Pete	19 secs	4th	Amir	44 secs
2nd	Jodi	26 secs	5th	Emily	49 secs
3rd	Jill	37 secs			

Join each child to the correct place on the timeline.

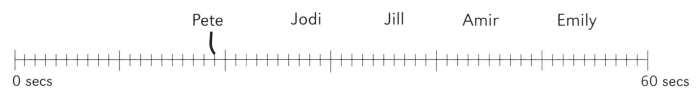

Answer the questions.

1 How much slower was Emily than:
   a) Amir? _____ b) Jill? _____
   c) Pete? _____

2 How much faster was Pete than:
   a) Jodi? _____ b) Jill? _____
   c) Amir? _____

3 How much less than 60 seconds is each child's time?
   a) Emily _____ b) Amir _____
   c) Jill _____ d) Jodi _____
   e) Pete _____

4 Christian plays the game. His time is half Amir's time.
   a) What is his time? _____
   b) What position does he take on the scoreboard? _____

PHOTOCOPIABLE
© Hopscotch Educational Publishing 2002

Name_____   ▶ Timelines – Activity Sheet 6

The life of Henry VIII

1491	Henry VIII born
1509	Henry VIII becomes king; marries Catherine of Aragon
1533	divorces Catherine of Aragon; marries Anne Boleyn
1536	Anne Boleyn executed; marries Jane Seymour
1537	Jane Seymour dies
1540	marries and divorces Anne of Cleves; marries Catherine Howard
1542	Catherine Howard executed
1543	marries Catherine Parr
1547	Henry VIII dies
Edward VI becomes king

Use the timeline to help you answer the questions.

1   For how many years was Henry VIII alive? _____

2   For how many years did he reign? _____

3   How old was he when he became king? _____

4   To whom was Henry VIII married in 1541? _____

5   How many different wives did he have between 1535 and 1542?
    _____

6   For how many years was he married to Catherine of Aragon? _____

7   Edward VI died in 1553. For how many years did he reign? _____

Name_____   ▸ Timelines – Activity Sheet 7

Will's timeline: 1

Read Will's summary of his life.

I was born in May 1994.
My sister Kate was born in July 1996.
My Great-gran died in November that year.
I started school when I was four, in September.
We moved house in August 1999.
My brother Daniel was born in February 2000.
We got a dog in April 2001.
I won a Maths certificate in March 2002.

Label the events on Will's timeline. Make sure you write them in the correct place.

Make notes for a timeline about your own life. Think of at least eight important events to include.

I was born in

Make a timeline of your life.

PHOTOCOPIABLE
© Hopscotch Educational Publishing 2002

Name_____ ▸ Timelines – Activity Sheet 8

Will's timeline: 2

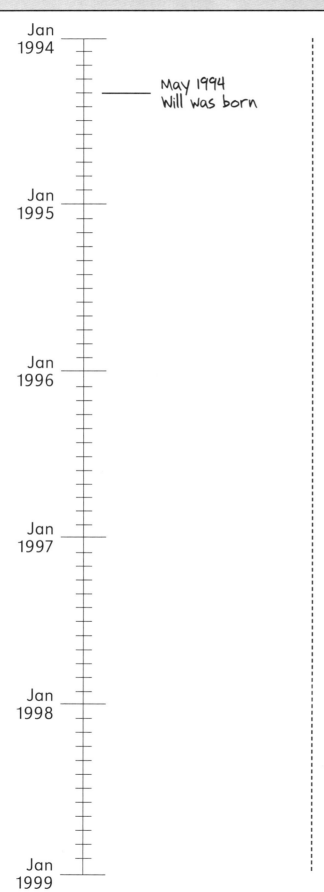

May 1994
Will was born

▸ Timelines and Timetables: Level 4

▸ UNIT 3: TIMELINES AND TIMETABLES
LEVEL 4

🕒 Learning objectives

- To estimate/check times using seconds, minutes, hours.
- To read and use timetables.
- To solve problems involving time.

Key vocabulary

- timetable, arrive, depart

🕒 Resources

- enlarged copies of a range of bus, train, coach and plane timetables

🕒 Introduction

- Show the children an enlarged copy of a simple bus timetable, showing buses between just two places. Ask them what information they can extract from the timetable, and ask them to calculate the time the bus takes to travel between the stops. Let the children explain their strategies for finding the answer. This could also be done using coach, plane or Eurostar timetables.

🕒 Activities

- **Activity Sheet 9** – Revise estimating time by asking the children to estimate the duration of particular journeys or activities, such as travelling to the nearest city. Discuss why it is important to be able to make estimates, for example if they are measuring how long something takes or making timelines they need to decide which is the best unit to use. Emphasise that for this activity it does not matter if they do not know exactly how long the things take. They should simply choose the most sensible answer. Give them the opportunity at the end to compare their answers with a partner, discuss any answers they do not agree on, and change their minds if they wish. As an extension, the children could make up more questions of this kind for a partner to solve.

- **Activity Sheet 10** – If necessary, revise the relationships between units of time, for example the number of weeks in a year, the number of years in a decade and so on. The children can work in pairs for this activity. Encourage them to work out the approximate length of each period of time by finding a near equivalent, for example 2400 hours would be 100 days, so 2500 hours is slightly more than 100 days. They can check their answers using a calculator. When put in the correct order, the letters spell out 'How long is a decade?' As an extension activity, you could ask the children to sort the cards according to whether each time period is more or less time than their age.

- **Activity Sheet 11** – Read the television guide with the children and discuss what time each programme begins and ends. Ensure that they understand that the film is shown in two parts. They may need to show their workings on another sheet of paper. After completing the activity, they could draw a timeline from 5 p.m. to 11 p.m. (or 17:00 to 23:00) and mark on the programmes. You could ask them to bring in real television guides and to work out how long their favourite programme lasts.

- **Activity Sheet 12** – Revise the key vocabulary: 'timetable', 'arrive' and 'depart'. Discuss the timetable with the children and ensure they understand how to read it. Check by asking 'What time does the first bus depart from Lake Road?' and 'What time does this bus arrive at the bus station?' The children could draw a timeline from 7:30 a.m. to 2:30 p.m. and mark on the times when the buses call at each stop.

- **Activity Sheet 13** – Read the airport screens with the children and explain that one shows details of planes arriving at the airport and the other shows planes departing. Point out that for questions 1 to 4 they will need to convert the 24-hour times to p.m. times. For drawing the timeline, the children could use Generic Sheet 4 (page 94). Each division on the timeline will represent five minutes and each copy of the sheet provides two timelines. The children could draw another timeline showing the airport arrivals.

▶ Timelines and Timetables: Level 4

- **Activity Sheet 14** – Each pair of children will need a copy of the train timetable on Generic Sheet 2 (page 92). Before they begin, look at the timetable together and ensure that they understand it. They will need to check each other's answers. When answering a question, they could write their answer on the back of the card, and it could be checked by a partner at the end of the game. More question cards could be made and added to the set, for a longer game.

- **Activity Sheet 15** – The children will need copies of the train timetable on Generic Sheet 2 (page 92). Before they begin, look at the timetable together and ensure that they understand it. They can use any part of the timetable to work out the time between stations, since each train takes the same amount of time. Explain that for the new timetable the journey still takes the same amount of time, but the trains run at different times.

- **Activity Sheet 16** – Use this activity when the children have completed the earlier timetable activities in this Level. Explain that in this timetable the trains take different amounts of time to travel between stations. Also point out that the trains do not all stop at all the stations. The children can bring in real timetables and write their own questions based on the timetables for a friend to answer.

- **Activity Sheet 17** – Once the children have joined the animals to the number line, they can count on and back along the line to help them answer question 1. Help them to work out strategies for solving the problems, using multiplication and division.

Support

Give the children copies of Generic Sheet 2 (page 92). Number the trains along the top 1 to 7 and explain that it shows seven trains running between Cherryton and Oaton. Set them simple questions based on the timetable, for example 'What time does train 1 stop at Appleton?', 'What time does train 6 arrive at Oaton?' and 'Write the time each train stops at Woolton.'

Challenge

In Activity Sheet 11, change the times on the television guide to 24-hour times.

After the children have completed Activity Sheet 12, give them several times for when the bus stops at Canal Street in the afternoon (these could be times to the nearest minute rather than to five minutes). Ask them to complete the timetable.

Ask the children to find out how long their favourite television programme lasts, then ask them to work out how long they spend watching it in one week, four weeks and one year.

Plenary

Obtain a local bus or train timetable. Enlarge it and/or make an OHT. Make true or false statements about the duration of journeys from one place to another, or at what time the bus or train calls at specific places. Ask the children to say whether the statements are true or false. They could respond by giving thumbs up for true and thumbs down for false.

Display opportunity

Make a chart showing journey times by coach from one particular city to various other cities around Britain. Write on the departure time for each coach and ask the children to fill in the arrival time at the destination. This could be done on a laminated surface so that it can be wiped clean and reused.

From London to:	Departs	Arrives	Departs	Arrives
Bath (3 hrs 15 mins)	07:45		08:25	
Bristol (2 hrs 20 mins)	08:20		09:05	

Extra activities

Copy and laminate the cards on Generic Sheet 1 (page 91). Ask the children to match each time period card to a suitable unit. Many of the time periods can be measured in a choice of units; challenge them to find a match for each unit of time.

Timelines and Timetables: Level 4

Answers

Activity Sheet 9

1. a) 2. b)
3. b) 4. c)
5. a) 6. a)
7. c) 8. b)

Activity Sheet 10

How long is a decade?

Activity Sheet 11

1. a) 35 mins
   b) 1 hr 15 mins
   c) 55 mins
   d) 2 hrs 15 mins
   e) 35 mins
2. 2 hrs 10 mins
3. 4:25 a.m.
4. 2 hrs 20 mins
5. 7 hrs 30 mins

Activity Sheet 12

1. 35 mins
2. 1 hr 20 mins
3. 30 mins
4. 10:50 a.m.
5. 2:15 p.m.
6. Canal St 7:55 a.m. 9:15 a.m. 10:35 a.m.
   11:55 a.m. 1:15 p.m.

Activity Sheet 13

1. 3:45 p.m.
2. 5:33 p.m.
3. 3:12 p.m.
4. 2:36 p.m.
5. 1 hr 21 mins
6. 24 mins
7. 1 hr 25 mins

Activity Sheet 15

Cherryton – Appleton	13 mins
Appleton – Wheaton	23 mins
Wheaton – Plumton	21 mins
Plumton – Woolton	14 mins
Woolton – Lambton	36 mins
Lambton – Cornton	19 mins
Cornton – Oaton	15 mins

New timetable:

Cherryton	07:24	10:53	13:24	15:53	18:24
Appleton	07:37	11:06	13:37	16:06	18:37
Wheaton	08:00	11:29	14:00	16:29	19:00
Plumton	08:21	11:50	14:21	16:50	19:21
Woolton	08:35	12:04	14:35	17:04	19:35
Lambton	09:11	12:40	15:11	17:40	20:11
Cornton	09:30	12:59	15:30	17:59	20:30
Oaton	09:45	13:14	15:45	18:14	20:45

Activity Sheet 16

1. 1 hr 36 mins
2. 1 hr 15 mins
3. 5
4. 09:15 from Eastley
5. 08:20
6. 10:36
7. 18 mins

Activity Sheet 17

1. a) 1.4 secs
   b) 2.1 secs
   c) 5.7 secs
2. a) 12.6 secs
   b) 31.5 secs
3. a) 300 m
   b) 800 m
4. a) 0 min 35 secs
   b) 1 min 3 secs
   c) 1 min 17 secs
   d) 1 min 32 secs
   e) 1 min 38 secs

Name_____ ▸ Timelines – Activity Sheet 9

Make an estimate

You can make a timeline to show how long activities or events take. First you need to estimate how long they take. Tick the best estimate for each of the following.

1 read a newspaper
   a) 30 minutes ☐
   b) 5 minutes ☐
   c) 2 hours ☐

2 train journey from London to Edinburgh
   a) 12 hours ☐
   b) 5 hours ☐
   c) 2 hours ☐

3 walk a kilometre
   a) 5 minutes ☐
   b) 15 minutes ☐
   c) 50 minutes ☐

4 boil a kettle
   a) 10 seconds ☐
   b) 1 minute ☐
   c) 10 minutes ☐

5 walk round the school grounds
   a) 10 minutes ☐
   b) 120 seconds ☐
   c) 50 minutes ☐

6 fly from Manchester to New York
   a) 3 hours ☐
   b) 14 hours ☐
   c) 8 hours ☐

7 make a paper aeroplane
   a) 30 minutes ☐
   b) 10 seconds ☐
   c) 5 minutes ☐

8 walk up a flight of stairs
   a) 10 seconds ☐
   b) 2 seconds ☐
   c) 60 seconds ☐

PHOTOCOPIABLE
© Hopscotch Educational Publishing 2002

Name_____   ▶ Timelines – Activity Sheet 10

Mystery phrase game

Cut out the cards. Put the cards in order of time, smallest to largest, to make a timeline.

The letters in the circles will spell out a phrase.

9 years **D**	500 weeks **E**	240 hours **L**
1 year **S**	200 weeks **D**	4000 days **?**
half a decade **C**	2 weeks **O**	1 week **W**
6000 minutes **H**	2300 hours **G**	30 months **A**
4 years **E**	100 days **I**	110 hours **O**
16 days **N**	2500 days **A**	

PHOTOCOPIABLE
© Hopscotch Educational Publishing 2002

Name_____   ▶ Timelines – Activity Sheet 11

What's on telly?

Read the television guide.

Channel 1

Albert Street	5:05 p.m.
Search for a Star	5:40 p.m.
Friends in Trouble	6:55 p.m.
Film: Thunderbolt	7:50 p.m.
News	9:00 p.m.
Film: Thunderbolt (conclusion)	9:35 p.m.
Championship Golf	10:40 p.m.

Answer the questions.

1   How long is each programme?
    a) Albert Street _____
    b) Search for a Star _____
    c) Friends in Trouble _____
    d) Thunderbolt _____
    e) News _____

2   If you watch Search for a Star and Friends in Trouble, how long is this?
    _____

3   Championship Golf is on for 5 hours 45 minutes. What time does it finish? _____

4   If you watch Albert Street four times a week, how long is this per week?
    _____

5   If you watch Search for a Star once a week for 6 weeks, how long is this? _____

Name_____   ▶ Timelines – Activity Sheet 12

Which bus?

Look at the bus timetable.

Lake Road	8:10 a.m.	9:30 a.m.	10:50 a.m.	12:10 p.m.	1:30 p.m.
Bus station	8:45 a.m.	10:05 a.m.	11:25 a.m.	12:45 p.m.	2:05 p.m.

Answer the questions.

1 How long does each bus journey take? _____

2 How long is there between one bus and the next? _____

3 You arrive at Lake Road bus stop at 11:40 a.m. How long will you wait for a bus? _____

4 You need to be at the bus station by 11:30 a.m. What time is your bus from Lake Road? _____

5 The 1:30 bus is 10 minutes late. What time will it arrive at the bus station? _____

6 The bus stops at Canal Street before it goes to Lake Road. It takes 15 minutes between these two stops. Fill in the rest of the timetable.

Canal St	7:55 a.m.	_____	_____	_____	_____
Lake Road	8:10 a.m.	9:30 a.m.	10:50 a.m.	12:10 p.m.	1:30 p.m.
Bus station	8:45 a.m.	10:05 a.m.	11:25 a.m.	12:45 p.m.	2:05 p.m.

Name _____ ▶ Timelines – Activity Sheet 13

Flight times

Look at the airport screens.

Arrivals	
Time	From
14:14	Athens
15:45	Nice
16:09	Madrid
16:18	Glasgow
17:33	Lisbon
18:28	Prague

Departures	
Time	To
14:36	Madrid
15:12	Stockholm
15:51	Munich
16:49	Prague
17:01	Bonn
17:43	Pisa

Answer the questions.

1   What time does the plane from Nice arrive?
    _____ p.m.

2   What time does the plane from Lisbon arrive?
    _____ p.m.

3   What time does the plane to Stockholm depart?
    _____ p.m.

4   What time does the plane to Madrid depart? _____ p.m.

5   It is 14:30. You are travelling to Munich. How long do you have to wait? _____

6   It is 13:50. You are meeting someone arriving from Athens. How long do you have to wait? _____

7   You arrive at the airport on the flight from Glasgow. You are travelling on to Pisa. How long do you wait between flights?
    _____

8   Draw a timeline showing all the airport departures.

PHOTOCOPIABLE
© Hopscotch Educational Publishing 2002

Name_____ ▸ Timelines – Activity Sheet 14

Train journeys

You need a copy of the train timetable.

Cut out the cards. Take turns with a partner to pick a card.

Use the timetable to answer the question.

If you are correct, keep the card. Who collects the most cards?

How long is the journey between Cherryton and Appleton?	How long is the journey between Woolton and Oaton?
How long is the journey between Wheaton and Cornton?	How long is the journey between Appleton and Oaton?
How long is there between the first train and the last train from Cherryton?	How long is there between the first train and the second train from Cornton?
What time does the earliest train depart from Lambton?	You are on the 09:48 from Cherryton. What time will you arrive at Plumton?
You are on the 15:59 from Woolton. What time will you arrive at Cornton?	What time does the latest train depart from Cherryton?
It is 09:32. You are at Appleton. What time does the next train depart?	It is 18:18. You are at Woolton. What time does the next train depart?
It is 11:56. You are at Wheaton. What time does the next train depart?	It is 14:23. You are at Cornton. What time does the next train depart?

PHOTOCOPIABLE

Write a timetable

You need a copy of the train timetable.

Write how long the journey takes between these stations.

Cherryton – Appleton _____

Appleton – Wheaton _____

Wheaton – Plumton _____

Plumton – Woolton _____

Woolton – Lambton _____

Lambton – Cornton _____

Cornton – Oaton _____

Next year the timetable is changing. Use the times above to help you write the new timetable.

Cherryton	07:24	10:53			
Appleton				16:06	
Wheaton			14:00		
Plumton					
Woolton					19:35
Lambton					
Cornton					
Oaton					

> Timelines – Activity Sheet 15

Name_____   ▸ Timelines – Activity Sheet 16

Take the train

Look at the train timetable.

Eastley	08:20	09:15	10:20	11:30
Thornton	08:36	09:28	10:36	11:45
Greenfield	08:50	—	10:50	—
Hepton	—	—	10:57	—
Oldbridge	09:17	10:05	11:22	12:29
Potton	09:45	10:33	11:53	13:00
Hazelford	09:56	10:44	12:10	13:11

1   How long does the 08:20 from Eastley take to reach Hazelford?
    _____

2   How long does the 11:45 from Thornton take to reach Potton?
    _____

3   How many stations does the 09:15 from Eastley visit altogether? _____

4   Which is the fastest train from Eastley to Hazelford?
    _____

5   You have to be in Hazelford by 10:00. Which train should you catch from Eastley? _____

6   You have to be in Oldbridge by 11:30. Which train should you catch from Thornton? _____

7   You are in Potton at 10:15. How long will you have to wait for the next train to Hazelford? _____

PHOTOCOPIABLE
© Hopscotch Educational Publishing 2002

Name_____ ▸ Timelines – Activity Sheet 17

Animal Olympics

These are the finishing times in a 100-metre race.
Join them to the correct place on the timeline.

| cheetah | wolf | dragonfly | elephant | human athlete |
| 3.5 secs | 6.3 secs | 7.7 secs | 9.2 secs | 9.8 secs |

```
0    1    2    3    4    5    6    7    8    9    10
                         seconds
```

Answer the questions.

1   How much faster was:
    a) the wolf than the dragonfly? _____
    b) the dragonfly than the human? _____
    c) the cheetah than the elephant? _____

2   How long would the wolf take to run:
    a) 200 m? _____   b) 500 m? _____

3   How far could the cheetah run in:
    a) 10.5 seconds? _____   b) 28 seconds? _____

4   If the animals kept up the same speed over 1 km,
    how long would each take?
    Write the answer in minutes and seconds.
    a) cheetah _____   d) elephant _____
    b) wolf _____   e) human _____
    c) dragonfly _____

▶ Timelines and Timetables: Level 5

▶ UNIT 3: TIMELINES AND TIMETABLES
LEVEL 5

Learning objectives

- To solve problems involving time.
- To examine events over set periods of time (year, century, millennium).

Key vocabulary

- year, century, millennium

Resources

- reference books on history and the Solar System

Introduction

- Show the children timelines from history books and discuss how long ago certain periods in history took place, for example the rule of the Romans in Britain and the Tudor period. Talk about why timelines are useful when investigating the past. Review the key vocabulary and ask the children to name major events that took place in the last year, last century and last millennium. Discuss how to find out about events in history and make a list of all the sources that can be used.

Activities

- **Activity Sheet 18** – Before beginning the activity, revise finding the difference between times. The children could do the activity in pairs. As an extension, they could collect information from local cinemas and set questions for each other based on the information.
- **Activity Sheets 19 and 20** – Use these activity pages together. Revise the terms 'century' and 'millennium' and ask the children when this century/millennium will end. Explain briefly what a comet is, or ask the children to find out for themselves using reference books. When they have worked out some of the dates, they should notice a pattern which will enable them to complete the rest without calculating.

  For the timeline, ask the children to first work out what each division on the line represents. They could mark on all the century divisions. Once completed, the sheet can be cut in half along the dotted lines and one half placed beneath the other to make a continuous timeline. Ask the children to work out how old they will be when the comet next appears. They could find out more about Halley's Comet using reference books, CD-ROMs and the Internet. They will find that the actual dates of sightings of the comet differ slightly from their own approximations.

- **Activity Sheet 21** – Briefly introduce the Solar System and the movement of the planets, or let the children research it for themselves using reference books, CD-ROMs and the Internet. Explain that Earth takes $365\frac{1}{4}$ years to travel once around the Sun, and this is why our year lasts for 365 days, and for 366 in a leap year. Show them pictures of the planets in relation to the the Sun and explain that each planet follows its own path around the Sun, called its orbit. Then discuss the chart and the graph on the activity sheet. Point out that the numbers on the chart have different numbers of decimal places. After completing the sheet, they could make a large timeline from 0 to 250 Earth years, and write (in approximately the correct place) the name of each planet and the duration of its year. Pictures of the planets could also be glued on.

- **Activity Sheet 22** – Use this activity after the children have completed Activity Sheet 21. They will need the chart and completed graph for reference. Encourage them to calculate mentally where possible, and to show all written workings on a separate piece of paper (it may be appropriate for some children to use a calculator). Point out that in questions 6 and 7 approximate answers are required, so they can round the figures up or down as necessary to simplify the calculations. For question 8, explain that they must choose which timeline to use for each period of time. Encourage them to first work out what the divisions on the

Timelines and Timetables: Level 5

timelines represent.

- **Activity Sheet 23** – Ask the children what each division on the vertical axis represents (£20) and ensure that they understand how to read the graph. Further questions could be set about how much money was raised by the school over certain periods of time.

Support

For Activity Sheet 20, the children could make a timeline on a larger scale, with each division representing 10 years instead of 20 years. This could be done using two copies of Generic Sheet 5 (page 95). Before photocopying, label the timeline at 100-year intervals (from AD 1000 to AD 3000).

Challenge

Ask the children to use reference books, CD-ROMs or the Internet to find out the length of a day for each of the planets in the Solar System (the time a planet takes to rotate once on its axis). They can draw their own chart and graph for the data they find, using the ones on Activity Sheet 21 as a model. They can then calculate the difference between an Earth day and the duration of each planet's day. They could also draw a timeline showing the planets which have days with a duration close to that of Earth.

Plenary

Use the chart on Activity Sheet 21. Ask the children to work in pairs, using a calculator and a whiteboard. Ask questions based on the data in the chart, for example 'How many Earth years in 3 Pluto years?', 'How many Earth years in half a Neptune year?' and 'How many Earth years in one Mars year?' Encourage the children to find the most efficient method possible and to show their method and answer on the whiteboard.

Display opportunity

Make a display of aspects of life in the past, using a chart with the headings 'One millennium ago', 'One century ago' and 'One year ago'. Ask the children to research aspects such as transport, food, homes, toys and buildings, using reference book, CD-ROMs and the Internet. Invite them to contribute pictures, cutting, drawings and their own writing to the display.

Extra activities

Using the cards on Generic Sheet 3 (page 93), the children can order events in history, work out how long ago particular events were, and find the number of years between two events. They could make a timeline of the millennium and glue on the cards in the correct places. Extra cards can be made for other events that the children have studied.

Answers

Activity Sheet 18

1. 2 hrs 15 mins
2. 12:30 14:45 17:00 19:15 21:30 23:45
3. 35 mins
4. 15:20
5. 10:25 12:45 15:05 17:25 19:45 22:05

Activity Sheet 19

1986	1461	2016	2586
1911	1386	2136	2661
1836	1311	2211	2736
1761	1236	2286	2811
1686	1161	2361	2886
1611	1086	2436	2961
1536	1011	2511	

1. a) 1 b) 13
2. a) 2 b) 14
3. 1000s, 1300s, 1600s, 1900s, 2200s, 2500s, 2800s

Activity Sheet 22

1. 2
2. 5
3. 1648 Earth years
4. 59.3 Earth years
5. 11
6. 6
7. 4

Activity Sheet 23

1. £360
2. £130
3. July
4. 5 months
5. 9 months
6. £80
7. £140
8. £640

Name_____   ▸ Timelines – Activity Sheet 18

Cinema times

Read the notice at the cinema.

SCREEN 1
THE LOST CITY NOW SHOWING AT:
10:50   13:05   15:20   17:35   19:50   22:05

Answer the questions.

1 How long is there between the start of one showing and the start of the next? _____

2 The film lasts for 80 minutes, with an extra 20 minutes of adverts at the start. Write the finish times for each showing.
_____ _____ _____ _____ _____ _____

3 For how long is the cinema empty between showings?
_____

4 You need to have finished watching the film by 6:40 p.m. What time is the latest showing you can see? _____

5 Screen 2 is showing Day of Destiny. There are 2 hours and 20 minutes between the start of one showing and the start of the next. Fill in the notice.

SCREEN 2
DAY OF DESTINY NOW SHOWING AT:
10:25   _____ _____ _____ _____ _____

PHOTOCOPIABLE
© Hopscotch Educational Publishing 2002

Name_____   ▸ Timelines – Activity Sheet 19

Halley's Comet

Halley's Comet orbits the Sun roughly every 75 years. The last time it appeared was in 1986. The next time will be in 2061.

Work out the approximate dates in the past when Halley's Comet appeared.

Work out the approximate dates in the future when Halley's Comet will appear.

1986   _____   2016   _____

_____   _____   _____   _____

_____   _____   _____   _____

_____   _____   _____   _____

_____   _____   _____   _____

_____   _____   _____   2961

_____   1011   _____   _____

Mark the dates on the Halley's Comet timeline.

Answer the questions.

1 How many times will the comet appear:
   a) this century? _____ b) this millennium? _____

2 How many times did the comet appear:
   a) last century? _____ b) last millennium? _____

3 List the centuries when the comet appeared/will appear twice in the same century.

_____

Halley's Comet timeline

Appearances of Halley's Comet

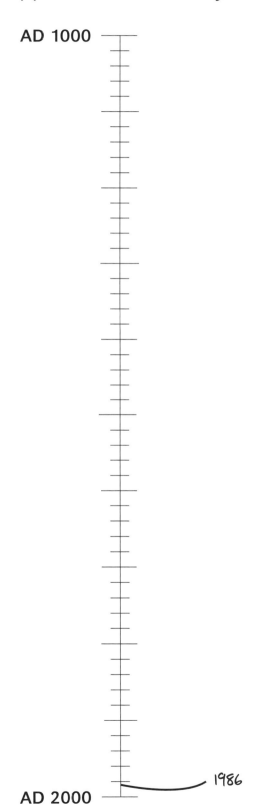

Appearances of Halley's Comet

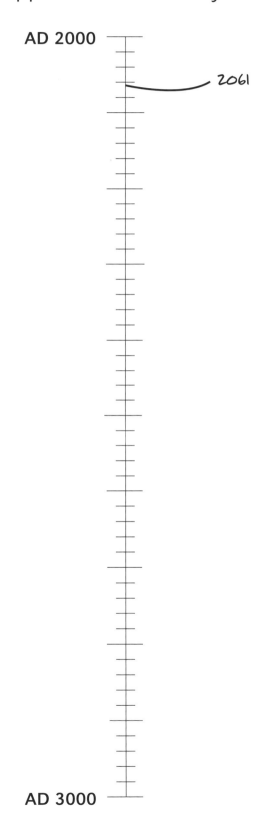

Name_____   ▶ Timelines – Activity Sheet 21

Solar System graph

A year is the time a planet takes to travel once around the Sun. Different planets have years of different lengths.

The chart shows how long a year is on each planet in the Solar System.

Planet	Duration of year
Earth	365.25 Earth days
Jupiter	11.86 Earth years
Mars	687 Earth days
Mercury	88 Earth days
Neptune	164.8 Earth years
Pluto	248.5 Earth years
Saturn	29.46 Earth years
Uranus	84 Earth years
Venus	225 Earth days

Be careful! Some are given in Earth days and some in Earth years.

Complete the bar chart.

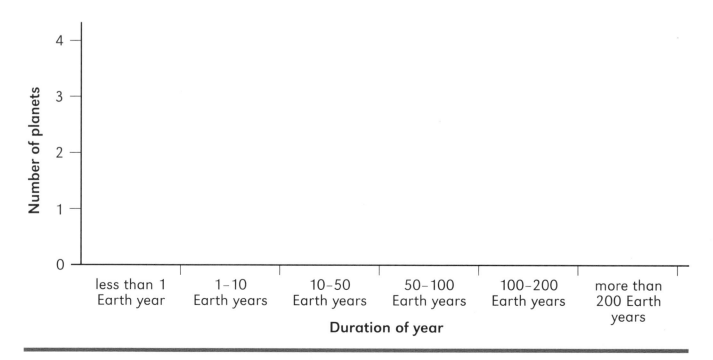

PHOTOCOPIABLE
© Hopscotch Educational Publishing 2002

Name_____   ▸ Timelines – Activity Sheet 22

Solar System questions

Use the charts to help you answer the questions.

1 How many planets have a year lasting less than 1 Earth year?
   _____

2 How many planets have a year lasting more than 10 Earth years?
   _____

3 How long will it take Neptune to travel 10 times around the Sun?
   _____

4 How long will it take Jupiter to travel 5 times around the Sun?
   _____

5 In 2475 Earth days, how many times will Venus travel around the Sun?
   _____

6 In 180 Earth years, approximately how many times will Saturn travel around the Sun? _____

7 In 1 Earth year, approximately how many times does Mercury travel around the Sun? _____

8 Mark the approximate length of each planet's year on one of these timelines.

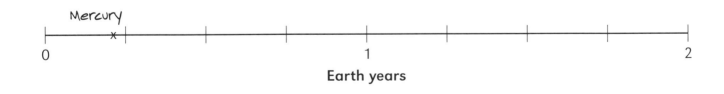

PHOTOCOPIABLE
© Hopscotch Educational Publishing 2002

Name_____   ▸ Timelines – Activity Sheet 23

Fund-raising

Oakcliffe School raised money for charity. The graph shows how much they raised over one year.

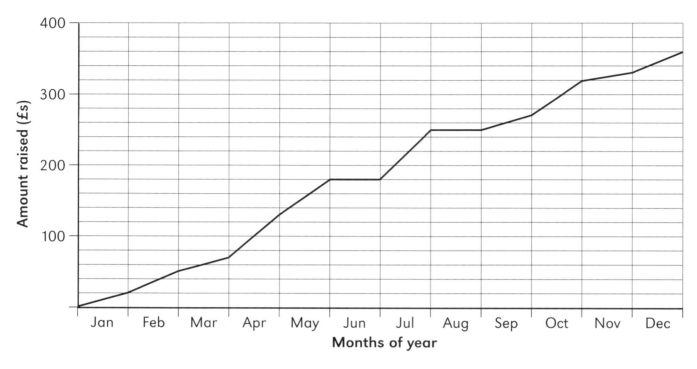

Answer the questions.

1 What was the total amount raised? _____

2 How much had been raised by the end of April? _____

3 In which month was £70 raised? _____

4 How long did it take to raise half the total amount? _____

5 How long did it take to raise three-quarters of the total amount?
   _____

6 How much was raised in March and April? _____

7 How much was raised between 31 May and 31 October? _____

8 The target is £1000. How much more does the school need to raise?
   _____

PHOTOCOPIABLE
© Hopscotch Educational Publishing 2002

Name_____ ▸ Timelines – Generic Sheet 1

Time estimates

the age of an oak tree	how long you spend asleep each year	how long it takes to fly from the UK to South Africa
how long it is until Christmas	how much holiday you have each year	how long it is since the Romans ruled Britain
how long it takes to brush your teeth	how long you spend travelling each day	how long it takes to cross the road
how long you spend at school each day	how long it is since World War II	how long it takes to eat breakfast
how long it takes to travel to the nearest town centre	how long it takes to put on your shoes	how long it is until August
seconds	minutes	hours
days	weeks	months
years	decades	centuries

PHOTOCOPIABLE
© Hopscotch Educational Publishing 2002

Train timetable

Cherryton	07:11	09:48	12:11	14:48	16:11	17:48	19:11
Appleton	07:24	10:01	12:24	15:01	16:24	18:01	19:24
Wheaton	07:47	10:24	12:47	15:24	16:47	18:24	19:47
Plumton	08:08	10:45	13:08	15:45	17:08	18:45	20:08
Woolton	08:22	10:59	13:22	15:59	17:22	18:59	20:22
Lambton	08:58	11:35	13:58	16:35	17:58	19:35	20:58
Cornton	09:17	11:54	14:17	16:54	18:17	19:54	21:17
Oaton	09:32	12:09	14:32	17:09	18:32	20:09	21:32

Dates in history

1870 Education Act	**1666** Great Fire of London
1914 Start of World War I	**1837** Victoria becomes queen
1509 Henry VIII becomes king	**1903** First powered aeroplane
1605 Gunpowder Plot	**1215** Magna Carta
1825 First regular rail services begin in northeast England	**1664** Great Plague begins
c. 1167 Oxford University founded	**1660** Samuel Pepys begins his diary
1066 Battle of Hastings	**1349** The Black Death
1580 Drake sails around the world	**1876** Telephone invented
1939 Start of World War II	**1477** First book printed in England
1564 William Shakespeare born	**1753** British Museum founded

Name_____   ▸ Timelines – Generic Sheet 4

Yearly/hourly timeline

PHOTOCOPIABLE
© Hopscotch Educational Publishing 2002

Name_____   ▸ Timelines – Generic Sheet 5

100- or 1000-year timeline

PHOTOCOPIABLE
© Hopscotch Educational Publishing 2002

Name _____

My Assessment Sheet

Name: _____ Date: _____

Main learning objective: _____

_____
(teacher to fill in before copying)

I can do this work: with support   ☐

                      independently   ☐

                      with an extension   ☐

I have learnt to _____

_____

Favourite activity
I really enjoyed _____

_____

Most challenging activity
I need more practice in _____

_____

My next target
I want to get better at _____

_____

PHOTOCOPIABLE
© Hopscotch Educational Publishing 2002